Praise & Acclaim

"Lianne shares an amazing love story with us. She fluidly walks us through the phases of her difficult yet beautiful relationship with her husband, taking us on their emotional roller coaster through the many joys and hardships they experienced as a couple, and finally relating the spiritual growth that she gained as a result. Her memoir reminds us how nothing is without reason. *Love Will Keep Us Alive* is a must-read for anyone who has lost a life partner to the other side and for anyone in general who questions if there is in fact 'another side.'"

Sherry Nash, Love Coach

"I was totally drawn into Lianne's magical love story and taken on a ride filled with joy, sadness, elation and despair. I truly felt the ups and downs of the people in this memoir. I had a difficult time putting the book down as I was so intrigued by where the story was leading me. If you love romance, raw vulnerability, passion and soul conversations, you will love this book."

Sharon Cohen, Holistic Naturopath

"Lianne eloquently shares her story about deep love, raw pain and the resilience to survive her grief and turn it into her biggest awakening. This is a love story that transcends time and space. Her communications with her husband open us up to the knowledge that death is not the end of life – only life as we know it. A real page turner!"

Doris Schöneberg, Parenting and Spiritual Coach

"I highly recommend this book to anyone who has cared for and suffered the loss of a loved one. Having lost both my mother and my best friend to cancer and currently supporting my husband as he struggles with this horrible disease, I was deeply moved by Lianne's story. Lianne's reference to feeling as though suffering from PTSD in dealing with cancer's impact on her family profoundly resonated with me. Her authentic description of living with the realities and ultimately losing a loved one to this epidemic is a Godsend that will help others to cope or at least realize they are not alone in their feelings. Her ability to transform the experience into a positive life change is a true inspiration."

Debora Must, Mindfulness Coach and Shaman Practitioner

"Inspiring and full of hope, Lianne's book was one I couldn't put down. Every chapter took me on a part of her voyage with her husband, Bob, and into the depths of what it is to be human. Her emotionally raw openness had me living those moments of love and loss, hope and grief, strength and survival. It showed me that we, as human beings, can live through the worst of times, rebuild our lives, and come out stronger. And it made me realize that our loved ones are always there; we just have to look for the signs."

Storm Leutner, Health Coach

"*Love Will Keep Us Alive* explores love, loss and the immense healing and learning that comes with communicating across the veil. Lianne's conversations with Bob hold a deep vibration of authenticity, further proof that love does endure and that life after life awaits us all."

Andrea Courey, Author of Conversations with Chloe

"Lianne's ability to express her journey made me feel as though I was alongside her. I appreciate her courage to share her deepest inner emotions and awakening experiences. The book helped me to see that we all have crossroads in our life that are meant to guide us. Lianne has empowered me and will undoubtedly inspire others through her story to realize that we must find our purpose and live our life with passion. I can't wait to share *Love Will Keep Us Alive* with others."

Jackie Percs-O'Donnell, Owner of Golden Home Care

"*Love Will Keep Us Alive* is a celebration of a love so deep, of two souls so connected, their love crosses barriers of time and physical constraints to reveal a profound knowing. Lianne draws you into her world, conveying her life story so deftly, readers forget they are not reading fiction. Her experience of loss is so palpable and heavy, it brings readers to their knees and back up again with an underlying thread of lightness and hope. If we are to take away Lianne's lesson to be more vulnerable, to let ourselves be open and love wholeheartedly and authentically, we just may be able to awaken to our true life's purpose."

Tiffany Moffatt, Fitness Director

"It's a moving, significant memoir written from more than one voice, magically portraying a true story of how open hearts turn towards each other to survive and thrive through adversity. I am eternally grateful to have read *Love Will Keep Us Alive*."

Heather Reid, Career Strategist

"A poignant, authentic, fast-paced love story that grabs you from the start and, after you reach a certain point, I defy anyone to lay it down!"

Lynda Hofmann, Life Coach

Dear Sandra,
what an incredible light you
are. You have so much courage.
You have inspired us so much
this week. I thank you for that.
May love continue to
infuse your life with magic.
Love Leann

LOVE WILL
KEEP US
Alive

A Journey of Awakening
through Heartbreaking Loss
and the Alchemy of Love

Lianne Bridges

DESIGNING
Transformation

Cover design by Joelle Fhima Berdowski
Interior layout by Noah Adam Paperman
Cover Image by Zeina Abdul Karim
Author photo by Wanda Malfara

ISBN 978-1-9990565-0-6 (Print)
ISBN 978-1-9990565-2-0 (Digital)

To my beloved late husband, Bob, and our beautiful sons, Kaiden and Kerrsen — the three greatest teachers in my life.

Table of Contents

Acknowledgements

With deepest gratitude I acknowledge my great love, Bob Parkinson, for helping me to live and write our story. Bob helped me to evolve both emotionally and spiritually throughout our life together. He still guides me, helping me to shine my light a little brighter each day.

My enormous thanks to our dear sons, Kaiden and Kerrsen, who gave me the reason to find my way through grief. Thank you so much, Boys, for allowing me to share our family's personal story with the world so others may find their way, too.

I also feel so fortunate to have benefited and enjoyed the love and support of a big and boisterous Irish-Catholic family. My parents, Russ and Dale, were always there for me when they were alive. And I could not have made it through the most difficult time of my life without the unwavering support of my brothers and sisters, Tiffany, Cauleen, Bruce and Dwight, along with my brother- and sister-in-law, Jamie and Tina. I also thank my aunts and uncles – Karen, Gerry, Ed and Pauline – and cousins – especially Kim, Glenn and Jane – for always reminding my sons through kind words and actions that they are part of an extended family network filled with love and support.

I thank Judy Tellier and the rest of the staff at NOVA Hudson for the kind support they provided Bob during his final days and Carol Jonas with the Carousel bereavement support for helping the boys through such a difficult time in their lives. I feel such deep love and appreciation for Bob's mom, Elizabeth, who openly welcomed me into the family without judgment. Our mutual love for Bob created a unique bond between us. I appreciate Bob's brothers, Robin, Leigh and Chris, and their spouses for supporting our family throughout Bob's illness and for helping to keep Bob's memory alive for all of us. I would also like to send my gratitude to Bob's children, Kevin, Stacy and Kim. Though I may not have been the most welcomed addition to their lives, I have always loved and respected each one of them. They have each brought much joy and learning into my life.

It takes a village to raise a child. In my case it took two villages – one in the Montreal area and the other in Toronto – to raise two children. To my Toronto friends – especially Martine, Heather, Cheryl, Wendy and Tom – who traveled regularly to Montreal to give emotional support and to help out with my boys, I am sincerely grateful. In the Montreal region, I want to thank all the mother's helpers, especially Karen, Doris, Zeina, Carol, Graham, Daphne, Tim, Carolyn and Sue, who opened their homes to my boys and me and were there whenever I needed help. Thank you to Judy and the Circle of Friends who rallied to help my family in our time of greatest need. My gratitude also extends to my Spirit Circle whose members helped to nourish my soul and to nurse my heart back to health after it was broken. A special thanks to Debbie for helping me to communicate with Bob across the Divide and to learn ways to connect with my own intuitive abilities. And, a heartfelt thank you to my friend and colleague Don, who has always supported me, even when we had to close the consulting business we ran together so I could explore a different path.

A very special thank you goes to the best neighbors anyone could ever have: Jessy and Leonard. They have been my family's trusted confidants and fierce protectors, wonderful surrogate grandparents to my children, and the most thoughtful friends in helping me to maintain a large home and property without my life partner.

The book's completion is due in significant part to Julie Gedeon, my writing coach, editor and dear friend. Without her guidance, faith and continuous encouragement in me and my writing, my story would never have been written. She taught me the art and magic of storytelling. Her Writers' Kitchen provided the creative community and accountability I needed to turn my story into a published memoir. I am grateful to my companions in the Writers' Kitchen, namely Sandy, Corry, Valerie, Seema, Susan, Catherine, Shannon and Nikki, for their steadfast encouragement and honest feedback throughout the many rewrites. I would also like to thank Carolyn Boll for initially helping me to get this project off the ground many years ago.

My appreciation extends to the entire publishing team, especially Alexa Nazzaro for guiding me through the ins and outs of self-publishing. Thanks to the Costa Rica photo shoot team, especially Zeina Abdul Karim for making me look so dreamy, as well as to the cover designer, Joelle Fhima Berdowski, and the interior book designer, Noah Adam Paperman.

Last but not least, a big thank you to all the book's early readers – Andrea, Debora, Doris, Heather, Jackie, Lynda, Sharon, Sherry, Storm and Tiffany – who took the time to go through the manuscript and provide loving and helpful feedback.

Merci à tous!

Preface

Writing *Love Will Keep Us Alive* has been one of the most difficult yet rewarding projects of my life. The process of writing my story has allowed me to see my experiences from a greater perspective. It helped me to sit with my pain, acknowledge it, surrender to grieving, and ultimately find gratitude in the tremendous loss I had endured. This has been my path towards healing with keen personal insights, a higher wisdom and a positive direction and purpose for my life. It is my hope that this book will provide at least some of the same for others.

What I had once believed to be real was only a fraction of a much greater non-physical reality. Each one of us has access to this unlimited wisdom, inspiration and guidance. Understanding this gave me the clarity and courage to awaken to my life and potential.

I came to realize that love is energy. It gives and sustains life – physically, emotionally and spiritually. It binds us to one another, even beyond death. I also came to understand that there is a new paradigm of spiritual partnerships emerging in our time. In the past, individuals primarily formed long-term bonds to help assure their physical survival as a family. Nowadays, more than ever, our relationships – cordial, spousal, familial and even professional – offer unique opportunities to advance our cosmic understanding and evolve our souls. Unconditional love is the key that unlocks the full potential of these kinds of spiritual partnerships. It starts with the relationship we each have with ourselves – with genuine self-love. This has certainly been my journey and I believe it is the gift of possibility offered to each and every one of us.

Introduction

"Your purpose is hidden within your wounds."

— **Rune Lazuli**

This book is about the power of love to awaken us to our lives. It illustrates the road long traveled with many distractions, detours, and ostensibly insurmountable obstacles on the journey towards living one's true path. My own difficult yet miraculous journey started with my husband's seemingly untimely death. My profound grief over losing Bob was the catalyst for a deep awakening within me that is nothing short of mystical.

When I met Bob, it was the first time in my life that I let my heart lead. I consciously abandoned rational thought and let myself fall head over heels in love with him. Until then, I had lived my life from the neck up. A deep voice inside of my being urged me to let go, just this one time, to simply feel. As I did so, I felt my heart expand and, with it, my whole life and everything in it.

What I gained from taking a chance with my heart was a partner who saw me, the true me beyond my physical form, social status or personality quirks. What I saw reflected in his eyes was so beautiful. It spurred me to become that reflection. My husband's love called on me to be the best I could become, not the small separate self, but the higher me, the whole me. As I witnessed Bob handle not only the physical but emotional and psychological ravages of the disease that eventually took his life, my respect and admiration for him deepened. As each new challenge was thrown at him, he addressed it with such grace, openness and raw authenticity that my love continued to expand to heights I never imagined. I knew the perils of falling even deeper in love and the inevitable ensuing loss, yet I allowed myself to feel these emotions instead of closing off my heart. I knew from experience with him that allowing myself to love and feel deeply in spite of insurmountable odds was my only authentic path and the true direction for my soul.

I believe our story was written long before either of us was born, and this actually is the case for all of us. We make a commitment on a soul level to help awaken one another. Bob helped me throughout our lives together to mature emotionally and evolve consciously. What I realize now is that this commitment didn't die with him. My husband's love continued to draw me upwards to connect with my soul after his death, to be closer to him in some way. As I transcended to higher states of being, I was able to continue to feel his love and communicate with him. Grief was the cliff I had to scale for transcendence and his loving guidance was my sherpa to spiritual echelons previously hidden to me.

"Love will keep us alive" were the five words engraved inside our wedding rings, taken from the title of our favorite song by the Eagles. They were also the last words Bob spoke to me before he died. It's been many years since that day. I have learned that true love, like the one Bob and I shared and the love I have for my children, is unconditional. It never dies. It may change form and expression, but it continues, even beyond death. This kind of love is not dependent on how we act, what we say, the roles we play, what we have, or any other condition. Learning to cultivate this kind of love for myself and then for those around me (friend or foe) has helped me to move beyond merely coping and healing from loss to ultimately awakening to my life and its purpose. It's my hope that this book can inspire others to believe in their own path and begin living the life we are all meant to live — one of love, passion, fulfilment and magic.

Playlist

Music played a major role in Bob's life. While writing this book, I often heard a song in my head. I began to notice that each song reflected the feelings I was trying to convey at the time. Perhaps this was Bob inspiring me in his unique way. I decided to include each of these relevant song titles at the start of every chapter. The songs form a playlist that musically chronicles my journey.

Chapter 1: Smile — Nat King Cole

Chapter 2: Feels Like Home — Chantal Kreviazuk

Chapter 3: Lovers in a Dangerous Time — Barenaked Ladies

Chapter 4: Bad Timing — Blue Rodeo

Chapter 5: What a Wonderful World — Louis Armstrong

Chapter 6: Hold On — Sarah McLachlan

Chapter 7: Have You Ever Seen the Rain? — Creedence Clearwater Revival

Part 1

"Ancient lovers never forget the echo of each other's hearts.
An ocean of lifetimes may pass but still, in the end, your
heart will guide you home."

— Unknown

CHAPTER 1

Smile

Bob and I sat in our home office listening to the voice over the speakerphone deliver the news we had been anticipating for weeks. We prayed it would allow us to return to our normal lives. We feared the worst. I stood to lean over the phone, as if that would help to soften the blow somehow. My stomach was in a knot, my mouth dry with anxiety.

Dr. David Mulder was the voice on the other end. In the twilight of his career, he remained one of Montreal's leading thoracic surgeons. His forty years of working in Quebec, once the world's largest asbestos producer, also gave him the lesser-known distinction of being one of North America's leading experts on mesothelioma: a deadly form of cancer directly related to asbestos exposure.

Bob had begun to show signs of a serious health problem seven months earlier. The doctors initially thought his symptoms were the result of pneumonia. When his labored breathing and coughing didn't clear up, the doctors assumed pleurisy. In September 2007, a lung specialist ordered a battery of tests. When Bob started to recover and no signs of any disease appeared on the latest x-ray, the specialist declared that Bob had dodged a bullet.

While Bob's health further improved that fall, he remained lethargic. He attributed his fatigue to an earlier thyroid illness that required removing the gland and replacing its functions with hormone-producing medication. By Christmas, he was slowing down again.

A couple of days after Christmas, the dry cough and flu-like symptoms returned. Bob checked himself into the local clinic and within days was back in the lung specialist's office. This time the specialist wasn't as positive. The x-ray results were "SIGNIFICANT MASS." He arranged for an immediate appointment with Montreal's top lung surgeon. The speed of the medical community's response told us Bob's situation was serious.

By the time we met with Dr. Mulder a week later, Bob had already lost a lot of weight. His breathing was labored. He told me he felt as if he was drowning, which caused him to panic as he fought for air. We were relieved to learn that during a biopsy that had been scheduled as rush with Bob's health deteriorating so rapidly, Dr. Mulder would be able to drain some of the fluid that had built up around Bob's lung. During the procedure, Dr. Mulder opened up Bob's ribcage and removed part of the sac surrounding his left lung. He also drained almost a gallon of fluid that had been pushing against Bob's lungs, challenging his every breath.

Dr. Mulder would not provide a diagnosis immediately after the procedure, but indicated that the prognosis did not look good. Trying to spare us any undue suffering, he answered our questions with, "Let's wait for the biopsy results." His response was unnerving. All we could do was to wait, hope and pray.

Bob went through a grueling recovery during his stay in the hospital. While his breathing improved, the wounds from the operation were so severe that he needed two epidurals just to keep the pain at a tolerable level. Back at home a week later, he continued to improve and started to regain his appetite. While the doctors still wouldn't commit to a diagnosis, they offered a range of possibilities from tuberculosis to lung cancer to mesothelioma. We hoped for tuberculosis, the only curable disease on the list.

I scanned the Internet for answers, for hope. By far the worst possible scenario was mesothelioma. Very few people survived this disease. Life expectancy was measured in months, not years. I didn't share this with Bob. I think his own self-preservation methods had kicked into play, as he chose not to look on line until he had received the official diagnosis.

Finally, after three weeks of uncertainty, we received the surgeon's phone call. Seconds felt like hours as we waited to hear the diagnosis that might change our lives forever.

"Malignant mesothelioma," the somber voice on the other end declared.

My heart raced. Blood rushed into my ears. My knees buckled.

I felt like someone had just sucker-punched me in the stomach. I looked at Bob as he slumped in his chair. I hugged him, trying to provide comfort when none could be given. I struggled to get out the words trapped in my throat: "What does this mean?" Unfortunately, I knew all too well what it meant. The most optimistic estimations indicated a life expectancy of six to twelve months.

"What are my options?" Bob asked, not yet fully realizing the extent of the blow that he had just received.

"I don't think surgery is an option at this point," stated the surgeon.

"Why not?" Bob asked in shock.

"Because I don't think it will accomplish anything and will cause a lot of undue suffering," Dr. Mulder replied.

"Then what do we do?" I pleaded.

"I have scheduled you for a consult with the Oncology Lung Clinic next Thursday," he said. "You'll meet with a team that includes me as your surgeon, a radiologist and an oncologist. They will recommend a course of action. I am out of town next week, but you can meet with the other two doctors. I don't want you to wait until I return."

After we hung up the phone, Bob and I just looked at each other. The proud, full-of-life, positive man I loved so much was slouched in his chair, completely dejected. "I feel like I have just been handed a death sentence," he said. I knew he was right.

"Malignant mesothelioma... surgery is not an option..." The doctor's words echoed through my mind as Bob and I sat in our home office. Silence engulfed the house, like the eerie stillness that follows an earthquake. I scanned my body for the after-effects. I was still alive. I looked over at Bob; he was alive, too. *Good! What next? Breathe.* I exhaled and my chest filled with pain as if I had inhaled the doctor's words as toxic smoke. The pain rose from my chest, up through my neck and into my mouth. My throat constricted. I could hardly breathe. Tears welled up in my eyes.

Desperate for some sort of release from this nightmare, I looked to Bob. His head drooped as the weight of the news filled his thoughts. A tidal wave of love and compassion flowed through me towards him. I reached over and placed his face between my hands. I felt the day-old stubble and the warm skin that softened the distinctive edges of his defined jaw and cheekbones, and wondered how I could possibly live without him. I pulled his gaze up towards mine.

"I will be with you every step of the way," I said, trying to appear strong and reassuring. "You know I will do anything I can to help you. I love you beyond words." He gave me a half-hearted smile. In that moment I could almost hear the crack of my heart as it began to break.

"I feel so bad for the kids," I said as the tears fell down my cheeks. Our sons, Kerrsen and Kaiden, were only five and seven years old. The thought of them growing up without their loving father was unimaginable.

Bob looked at me tenderly and said, "I feel bad for us."

Crack! There went my heart again. We had such a beautiful relationship. I couldn't begin to imagine a life without Bob, my love, my soulmate, my everything... I didn't understand how this could be possible. I felt there had to be some huge mistake.

Disbelief eventually turned into confusion. *Now what? How could we solve the unsolvable?* I searched desperately for solutions. In the past, we had been able to find our way out of almost every difficult situation thrown our way, and there had been many. But we had never faced anything this insurmountable, this terrifying. I clung to one thought that gave me strength: we had each other and, together, we would face the dark times ahead.

My mind raced. *Who should know? What do we say to our boys? Oh, our poor sweet little boys! How would we break this horrible news to them? And Bob's mother? How would we inform her, and my own mom who was waiting downstairs?* "My mom must be wondering what's happening," I said.

Tentatively, Bob lifted himself from the chair. We walked downstairs and into the kitchen. The look on my face told her the news was not good. She immediately began to cry. My mother knew all too well the road that lay ahead of us. Ironically, a year ago to the day, she had lost my father – her husband of fifty-four years – to cancer. I hugged her tightly. My voice quivered as I whispered in her ear: "It looks like we are going to be widows together."

She pulled back and gave me a stern motherly look. "Never give up hope. You don't know what the future holds." Her words were delivered with great conviction and compassion. If only I could believe them. If only she could make this boo-boo go away as she had others when I was a child.

Bob's voice broke through the tension. "I better call Chris. He's only a couple of hours away. He can help me to tell my mom."

Bob's older brother was at his vacation home in the Adirondacks. Bob and his other brothers nicknamed Chris "the Pope" growing up, because he never did anything wrong, unlike Bob and his other two older siblings, Leigh and Robin. Chris was the one the family called upon in times of crisis.

Very few words were exchanged between Chris and Bob on the phone. "It doesn't look good," Bob said in a quiet voice. It awed me that he could muster up the courage to communicate anything while he was still himself processing the diagnosis. Crack! My heart was starting to shatter. Seeing his composure in the face of such a devastating prognosis deepened my love for him. The preciousness of this love made me fear losing him all the more.

"We decided to wait until he gets here to tell my mom," Bob explained as he hung up the phone.

Both drained, we sat on the couch, leaning on each other to anchor ourselves. Our first big purchase as a couple, the cream-colored sofa was unpractical with small children, but it had cushioned us while relaxing, entertaining, watching movies, cuddling, discussing family issues, reading to our boys, and now through our trauma.

"My mom knows, your brother Chris knows and is on his way... Now what?" I asked. With my pulse racing and stomach doing somersaults, I suggested we do something – anything – rather than sit and wait for his brother to arrive.

We decided to go shopping, as a distraction with a familiar comfort. Unfortunately, it had the opposite effect. Walking the aisles of the local big box store felt surreal. I drifted in a fog. Every item mentally hit me with our new reality. Party decorations made me realize that Bob would not be around to celebrate our sons' birthdays. Baseballs and footballs made me think about how Bob would not be able to share his love of playing sports with them, or his older son, Kevin. As I looked at the racks of children's clothes, sorted by age, the cruel reality that Bob would not see our children develop through the different stages of their lives began to take hold of me.

We drifted by the home decoration and appliance sections. For the first time since we had received the news, I realized that I would become a single parent and have to manage our household alone. "Oh, my God, how the hell am I going to do this by myself?" I cried. Bob held me in his arms. I felt weak and ashamed. *Pull it together, Lianne. You should be the one comforting him, and not the other way around.*

We ran into a neighbor by the women's fashion section. Bob and I shared a glance that asked whether we should walk the other way. It was too late. She smiled as she greeted us. I tried to smile back as we exchanged niceties. I fought back tears. It was so hard to hide the raw emotions that were rushing to the surface. I realized it was going to be tough informing all the people in our lives, not just the ones closest to us, but casual friends, colleagues and even mere acquaintances. I could see that each time we shared the news it would be painful. I did not want people to pity us. I was too proud to let others see me weak and vulnerable.

When we returned home, Chris was already there waiting, having jumped into his car right after Bob's call and driving a two-hour route across the border in record time. Chris had picked up Bob's mom on the way to our place. We were all concerned about how she would handle the news. While she was a vibrant ninety-one-year-old, we knew she would be devastated.

I held Bob's hand as I sat next to him on the couch. His mom sat on the chair facing him, anxious to know what he was about to share. "Mom, my doctor phoned today," Bob said as gently and lovingly as possible. "He gave me the biopsy results." Each pause between his words felt like an eternity. I could hear the clock ticking in the adjacent room.

"They think I have mesothelioma," he said. "A cancer associated with exposure to asbestos. My surgeon doesn't think it's operable."

For the second time in as many hours, I listened to Bob tell a loved one the news that he was just starting to come to grips with himself. Again, his gentle yet strong manner deeply touched me. *Crack, crack, crack!* My heart was not going to withstand much more of this. I looked into his mom's eyes. They reflected back such deep sadness for her youngest son, her baby. I could feel the loving bond they had shared for fifty-eight years. Bob and his mom were close. He had been the son who looked after her for the past two decades, as he was the only one still in Montreal.

As we discussed the surgeon's gloomy prognosis, Chris suggested we speak with Bob's family doctor. Surely she would have some words of wisdom to share. We called her office and were put through to her immediately. She knew that we had been waiting for the biopsy results. Like most people who met Bob, she was very fond of him. We could tell she wanted to help.

When we described the diagnosis, she gave us the first bit of encouragement.

"Never give up hope," she said. "I often see people who have been given very little chance of surviving make amazing recoveries. Just yesterday there was a woman in my office who was diagnosed with terminal ovarian cancer and given months to live twenty-five years ago. She bounced out of my office, healthy as a horse."

The tension eased slightly as we listened to her words. *Maybe we weren't so powerless after all,* I thought. *While we might not be able to control the cancer eating away at Bob, maybe we did have some choices. We could decide how to handle this crisis — by throwing in the towel or putting up a fight. We could decide on the direction of his treatment – aggressive or conservative, natural or traditional. Most importantly, we could decide what story we were going to tell ourselves. Did we see ourselves as victims of fate or warriors rallying with hope against insurmountable odds?*

It seemed positive thinking was the only thing we could do to turn our situation around. I wanted desperately to be a comfort to Bob and my children and also to feel stronger, more in control of the drama that was unfolding around me. I tried hard to smile even though my heart was breaking. *I can get through this. I have to. If not for me, for Bob and the boys.*

That call from Bob's doctor was the alarm bell from my higher self to begin a journey of self-awakening. There had been other nudges in the past, but this time I could no longer hit the snooze button.

CHAPTER 2
Feels Like Home

I had been working as a marketing manager at Nabisco's head office in Toronto for a few months when I experienced my first encounter with Bob. As Quebec regional sales director, Bob phoned me to ask why I hadn't produced the latest Oreo commercial in French for his market.

The voice I heard for the first time had the smooth depth of a late-night radio announcer. "You folks at head office always forget about us in Quebec, thinking the world revolves around the center of your universe," he said, poking fun at the centric stereotype of Torontonians.

"You mean it doesn't?" I teased back.

My experience with the sales department up to that point had not been pleasant. I worked in a department of young, mostly female marketers in a male-dominated business. We had to fight for everything. Most of the salesmen were significantly older and quite chauvinistic. "I'm so used to you Sales guys berating us here that I'm surprised you see the funny side of this!" I said. "We get so little respect... They even call us 'girls'!"

"Oh, I know. I hate being called 'a girl.' It's so derogatory." His kidding was all the more amusing with his deep male voice.

I laughed so loud that my cubicle neighbors started to take notice. I was intrigued by this faceless man on the other end of the line. It had been a long time since anyone had made me laugh like that, especially at work.

"And I particularly hate those blue dresses and hairnets they make us wear in the bakery. So unflattering," I joked back.

"I know what you mean. They add ten pounds, which doesn't help when you're eating cookies all day!"

I laughed wholeheartedly again. When I hung up the phone, I couldn't stop smiling and was more than a little bit curious to meet this guy in person. The opportunity arose a month later at a sales and marketing meeting. When I entered the large meeting room at the conference center, Bob stood on the far side facing in my direction but was absorbed in conversation with his manager.

I instantly knew it was him because he was the only person in the room I hadn't previously met. I took advantage of his being engaged in conversation to check him out. He was tall, about six feet, with a solid build. He looked to be in his mid-thirties. He wore a nondescript golf shirt and slacks, the casual business 'uniform' at that time.

When he noticed me looking at him, he stopped mid-sentence and a broad smile erupted across his face. He recognized me as the only woman in the crowd he hadn't met yet. He immediately concluded his conversation and made his way towards me.

"You must be Lianne," he said with assurance.

"Uh, yes. And you must be Bob?" I stuttered, offering my hand to shake, trying to act businesslike.

He took my hand and pulled me closer, kissing me on both cheeks, a Quebec custom familiar to me from growing up on Montreal's West Island. A shiver ran up my spine as I felt the heat of his body and inhaled the citrus of his aftershave. I stepped back, awkwardly. His crystal blue eyes seemed a mix of wisdom and playfulness. He wasn't the young, trendy urban kind of guy that I was used to dating, but there was something about him. An almost bald head and Roman nose gave him an air of distinction. His broad smile was accentuated by a cleft chin. His most notable feature, if it could be called that, was his presence. He exuded confidence and charisma. "So, you're 'the girl' from Marketing, eh?" he said, holding my gaze longer than business people should.

I laughed, remembering our first conversation. "Yes, and you didn't wear your blue dress today? Are you trying to avoid the stereotype?"

"Yes, and I left my hairnet at home." He rolled his eyes up towards his balding head with self-deprecating humor. "I didn't want to get pinched. The evening events can get quite out of hand when the Sales guys start drinking. Beware of that one in particular," he said, pointing to a senior sales director.

Over the following months, Bob and I came to know each other as colleagues and friends. Living in separate cities, we only saw each other occasionally at conferences and workshops. I enjoyed his company immensely and looked forward to us spending time together. We often went out for drinks or dinner in a group after a day's meetings, accompanied by his close friend at work and one of mine. The four of us would kid each other and laugh for hours, often exchanging aspects of each other's lives that were quite personal. It was at one of these gatherings that I learned he was thirteen years my senior. I was stunned. He didn't look or act that old to me. At that stage in my life I thought anyone over forty was over the hill.

About two years into our friendship, we both took part in an intensive leadership training course focused on managing change and transition. We participated in the same breakout groups, poking fun at each other throughout the sessions. When a group from the class discussed going out for dinner that evening, Bob took me by surprise when he quietly suggested: "How about we ditch these guys and go out alone?"

I probably should have noticed that he had been flirting with me. Maybe I was in denial. I wasn't a stranger to advances from men. By my mid-twenties, I already had a range of experiences with the opposite sex, including friendships, brief love affairs and longer relationships. But this was different. He was married, and had kids. Plus I was in a serious relationship. Yet I worried that if I turned him down, I would lose him as a friend.

Excitement mixed with anxiety as I considered his offer. "No, thanks. I have to get home," I finally replied in an unconvincing tone. "My boyfriend is waiting for me."

I had done the 'right' thing and yet I was exhilarated that Bob had asked me to dinner. My stomach was in knots during my whole drive home. My body was pumped full of adrenaline. *This is what it feels like to be alive. What do I do if he asks me again?*

I cared about my boyfriend, but our life together had become intellectually and emotionally flat. David (not his real name) was kind and fun-loving, but our interests differed. We hardly saw each other during the week because of our busy work schedules. On weekends, he was off early to play golf or some other sport, leaving me to look after the house and run errands. At first I considered our routines as typical of a good longer relationship and accepted being more like friends than lovers. Being with him was like enjoying the calm of gentle background music, but my dissatisfaction increased steadily after I met Bob. I knew I wanted more, but fear kept me from leaving. When Bob flirted with me, I felt noticed, appreciated, excited. Our conversations hit the wide range of notes that made my heart sing. I didn't know what I was missing until I found it.

From the moment Bob asked me to dinner, I couldn't get him out of my head. Excitement and desire filled my being, but judgment and fear controlled my thoughts. I told myself that under no circumstances would I get involved with a married business colleague. At the same time, I fantasized about getting closer to Bob. I suggested that we meet the next time I went to Montreal on business. *I just need to explain my intentions to him. I'll talk with him, explain that a relationship between us could never work.* I hoped that we could go back to the way things were between us, that we could still be friends. Of course, I could no more revert to our former relationship than a butterfly could slink back into her chrysalis.

A couple of weeks later, we met for breakfast to hold "the discussion." As soon as he entered the restaurant and looked at me, I could feel his pull. He angled his body in his seat to be closer to me. He looked right into my eyes as we talked, and hung on my every word. His total focus on me threw me off balance, lowered my resistance. I was lured by his attention, by feeling like I really mattered.

As always, he approached the situation with humor. "So, you want to talk about 'us,'" he said, with a grin that revealed perfectly straight teeth and mischievous dimples.

"No. Well, yes. I guess so," I stumbled.

I sensed that little had changed from his point of view. For me, everything had changed. "At the last workshop, you asked me to go out with you for dinner without the others… Why?"

He laughed at my directness. "I wanted to go to dinner with you!" He was not going to make this "discussion" easy for me. Clinking plates and the people chatting in the adjacent booth filled the awkward silence between us.

"Okay, let's say there were some feelings between us… I mean more than just friendly ones," I ventured. "What do you think we should do about it?"

"It's always important to 'express' your feelings," he replied in a tongue-in-cheek reference to one of the leadership workshop lessons. "I've heard that it isn't good to bottle them up."

I was torn between wanting to banter with him and getting my point across. "If we do 'express our feelings,' as you suggest, there could be consequences, personally and professionally."

"Not if no one finds out," he suggested with a twinkle in his eye.

Images of us together flashed through my mind. Desire spread throughout my being. I was losing more of my resolve with each passing moment.

"Where is your meeting today?" he asked, changing the subject.

"By the bakery." I had planned to attend some focus group sessions at a research house near the company's manufacturing facility.

"Why don't I give you a tour of the bakery after your meeting? I can pick you up."

I hated the possibility of our visit ending with breakfast and that I probably wouldn't see him until the next workshop in another month. Although conflicted, I agreed to meet with him later. The tour of the bakery turned into drinks. Drinks became dinner. We talked, laughed, joked and teased each other the entire time. I marveled at how we could go from 'nothing between us' to 'obviously something between us' in such a short time. Maybe there was always something there, but at the time I just knew that as much as my heart and body wanted this man, my brain warned me that I could be headed for real trouble.

We shared a scrumptious dinner at an Italian restaurant that my family frequented when I was young. I lived close by until I was seventeen and my father's company relocated to Toronto. A lot had changed in the fourteen years since I was last at the restaurant in the late seventies. I had finished high school, completed undergraduate and master degrees, and started my life as an adult with a job and responsibilities.

The restaurant had changed a lot, too. It had started out as a simple pizzeria with red-and-white checkered tablecloths. Over the years, it had evolved into a fine dining establishment with beautiful decor and trendy Italian dishes. The restaurant's transformation was mirroring my own. Bob's attention and obvious admiration had coaxed this butterfly out of her cocoon. Instead of being an awkward young girl, I felt sexy, confident, alluring.

Bob's voice was velvety, hypnotic. I hung on his every word. We sat inches from each other's skin. The sexual energy between us was palpable. I didn't want to miss a moment of this delicious experience. As much as my head told me to resist, the rest of my body did a free fall into his energetic vortex. I wanted the dinner to last forever, but I had to catch a plane back to Toronto. Reluctantly, we finished our meal and left the restaurant. I buttoned up my long teal coat and wrapped my cream scarf around my neck to protect me from the cold October air. We walked slowly towards his car, trying to make the night last as long as possible. He went to the passenger side of his station wagon to open the door for me. I was impressed by his gentlemanly manners, but felt a rush of guilt in the presence of such a visible reminder of his being a family man. I soon realized Bob had a selfish motive behind his chivalry. Holding the door for me provided him with the opportunity to go for a kiss.

For a moment, we both stood awkwardly shivering in silence. Bob pulled me close, encircling me in his arms. Without resisting, I slipped my hands into his coat. His body was like a radiator gently warming me. His tall, masculine stature arousing. I felt graceful and feminine in his powerful arms. He took my head in his hands and led me into our first kiss. His lips were soft. His tongue gently invited me to join his. My heart drummed in my ears. My chest heaved with each breath. Blood flowed throughout my body igniting every nerve. Excitement and desire coursed through my veins, hijacking all my control systems. Every fiber of my body screamed to let go, to abandon myself to this desire. Underneath the passion lay something much deeper: calmness, certainty, a knowing. It was as if I'd had amnesia and was beginning to remember a long forgotten love. It felt like home.

After several minutes, we released our embrace, laughing embarrassingly at such a public display. "I hope no one saw us," I said with a giggle and guilt.

"I feel like a teenager," Bob said as he looked around to see if anyone had noticed. He directed his glance to the house behind us. A sixties' bungalow. "I think George and Martha got quite a thrill," he joked. "This is probably the most action they've seen in years."

Both of us burst into awkward laughter. Throughout the day that we had spent together, I had felt such a tingling connection with him. At twenty-nine, I thought that I had finished growing up, that I had become the woman I was to be. Yet, on many levels, I was still a girl. I had been stuck in my safe cocoon. Like a caterpillar that couldn't imagine that it would fly one day, I could not see the passionate, spiritual being that lay dormant within me. While the blueprint for my evolution was embedded deep inside me, I needed a catalyst to trigger my transformation. Venturing out and testing my wings that day had been scary, but exhilarating. This small taste of flight made me feel totally alive. I wanted more. On some level I understood that the fictional bungalow couple that Bob and I imagined actually represented us, reawakening to our lives.

CHAPTER 3

Lovers in a Dangerous Time

Arriving home late from Montreal, I quietly crawled into bed so I wouldn't wake David. Early the next morning, the autumn sunlight beamed through our bedroom's large window, waking me before the alarm. The joys of the previous day filled my head. Bob and I had shared so much of ourselves — including our dreams and intimate details of our lives — within the few short hours we had spent together. I recalled Bob's arms wrapped around my body as he kissed me. Sexual longing stirred within me again, as it had the prior night. I looked at David sleeping next to me. He was a handsome man with his raven hair, blue eyes, chiseled features and six-pack abs that he loved to show off. I wondered why I wasn't attracted to him the way I now was to Bob.

David opened his eyes. "Hi, Lee Lee Bear! How was your trip?"

"Not bad." I jumped out of bed to avoid his eyes. "A lot of boring research... You know what it's like." I padded toward the bathroom, the hardwood creaking under my feet, as if saying: liar, liar!

"Yeah, I know. I hate those focus group sessions."

I had met David six years earlier during my interview for a marketing job at Campbell Soup. Senior management had asked him as a recent young hire to field any questions from the new business school graduates who were applying, as well as to assess each candidate's fit with the organization. I'm not sure whether David had any say in my being offered a position. I declined in favor of working for Unilever because it was recognized as the best training organization in Canada for marketing executives at the time.

A year later I ran into David at a marketing awards event. We immediately recognized each other. He poked fun at me for turning down his company, suggesting I was playing hard to get. We exchanged business cards, promising to keep in touch. I was surprised to receive a package at work from him the very next day. The box was filled with Campbell Soup bowls, cooking mitts and utensils. "Dear Snuggle Bear," the note said in playful reference to the mascot for Unilever's fabric softener. "Some gifts for your kitchen. Will you have drinks with me?"

Intrigued by David's quasi-romantic gesture and unique sense of humor, I agreed. His good looks and charm quickly won me over and we began seeing each other regularly. Four years into the relationship, we moved in together.

"Did you at least get a chance to grab a good meal downtown?" he asked from the bedroom. Being from a wealthy family, David had often driven from the Eastern Townships where he had worked as a tennis instructor during his younger summers to eat at Montreal's best restaurants.

"No, I just grabbed a bite close to the research facility," I replied, still brushing my teeth without facing myself in the mirror.

I walked into the kitchen and searched the refrigerator for some kind of breakfast. David's half of the fridge had only a bunch of carrots, a couple of soft drink cans, and leftover spaghetti in an unwrapped bowl. I rolled my eyes and pulled out a large jug of orange juice from my side. We bought everything separately, including groceries, because we regarded money so differently. He watched every penny. I loved to spend.

Rinsing a glass from the stack of unwashed dishes, I became irritated that David had once again left them for me to do. He probably had another late night with his study group. A few months earlier, David had left his position at Campbell Soup to return to school to earn his master's degree.

After pouring the juice, I glanced over to the dining area that opened into the living room. Hand-me-down furnishings from both our families decorated the spacious two-bedroom flat. We hadn't purchased anything as a couple, even after living together for more than a year. I felt like the furniture was content to coexist while patiently waiting for a better home.

Despair overcame me as I recognized the staleness of my day-to-day life. It felt like I had re-entered a black-and-white world after being shown a glimpse of one filled with color. *How can I possibly return to this life as if nothing happened? I can't unsee the colors.*

And yet I fully realized the unlikelihood of a future with Bob who had already told me that he had stayed married despite being unhappy.

Guilt added to my suffering. *I have betrayed David and seduced another woman's husband.* I pushed down my feelings of being a horrible person as I guzzled the orange juice and then rushed to take a shower.

I avoided speaking with David as I prepared to leave for work. I didn't trust myself. *I might cry, or worse, blurt out the truth.* Halfway out the door, I threw on my coat and called back over my shoulder at him to have a good day.

Driving to work I let my mind wander to when David entered my life. He felt like a safe harbor for my weary spirit about a year after a tumultuous period in my life. After five years together, however, I longed for more passion and adventure. If I pursued a relationship with Bob, I knew I would be wading back into rough waters. *Am I ready for that? Am I willing to open my heart with the likelihood that it will be broken when he chooses his marriage over me?* I looked for signs to help me decide. I didn't have to wait long.

I had a difficult time re-entering the land of black and white. Over the month leading up to my next meeting with Bob, I felt torn between immense anticipation and being riddled with fear and guilt. I couldn't stop thinking about him. I didn't eat or sleep well. I took long walks alone. I spoke to a couple of trusted friends, asking for advice. The week before Bob and I were to meet at the next course, I took a day to indulge in shopping. As I tried on a blouse, I wondered if Bob would like me in it. I lost myself in various fantasies of us being together as I shopped for hours. When I returned home that evening, I sensed immediately something was wrong. David asked me to sit down. *Oh, my God, did something happen to my parents?*

"Fatima was hit by a car," he said with compassionate eyes. I was relieved that it was not my parents, but my relief quickly turned to concern. I had become very attached to my cat over our 12 years together. "Is she all right?" I asked, looking around the apartment for her.

"She didn't make it. I'm sorry."

"No!" I fell back onto the bed.

"I tried to contact you. I went to your friends, but no one knew where you were." Cellular phones weren't yet commonly owned back then.

Sitting next to me, David took me in his arms as I sobbed. David had earlier put Fatima's body in a box until we could bury her at his parents' country place. He and his parents were so kind and supportive. I felt guilty taking him for granted. Here I was spending the day shopping and dreaming of Bob, while David had to deal with my cat and trying to find me.

I stayed awake in bed that night, mentally beating myself up. *I caused this. God or whoever is punishing me. It's a warning. I have to stop imagining a relationship with Bob and return to reality.*

The next day, an anxious knot formed in my stomach as I

drove to the hotel where our week-long course was being held. After check-in, I headed to the elevator to go up to my room. The doors swished open and Bob stood inside. My heart leaped. He looked up from the course agenda in his hand. A big smile lit up his face. "Hey, sugar!" he said, being almost too familiar as he greeted me with a kiss on both cheeks. "Why don't you drop your bags in your room, and we can grab a drink at a local watering hole?"

It's only a drink. It can't hurt. As long as I stay strong, nothing will happen.

We found a small pub a few blocks from the hotel. A couple of days before Halloween the place was decorated with cobwebs, ghosts and ghoulish pumpkins that reflected the vibe between us – shadowy and mischievous.

Seated across from me, Bob leaned closer. "I haven't stopped thinking about you since that night in Montreal," he whispered.

"Me neither," I said as I leaned back slightly. "But we can't do that again. It isn't right. We need to resist our feelings."

"How do you plan on doing that?" Bob looked at me with a comical laugh.

"We just have to be strong!"

After dinner, we went to my car. We both climbed in and I quickly buckled my seatbelt.

"Do you really think that will help?" Bob said as he leaned over to kiss me.

The touch of his lips melted my resolve. For a second time I felt this strange mix of passion arising from a new relationship along with the comfort and ease of a long-term friendship. *Lovers in a Dangerous Time* by the Barenaked Ladies played on the radio. I smiled at the coincidence. It was as if Bob and I were being called out for our crime – a crime of passion that I couldn't seem to stop myself from committing.

I pulled away. "We better get back to the hotel."

At the hotel elevator, I pushed the button. "It's late. I'm going to bed."

We rode up in silence, but the electricity between us was deafening.

"Goodnight," I said, rushing out the doors as they closed behind me.

Phew, I made it. How am I going to last a whole week like this?

The next morning, I met Bob at the coffee stand in the workshop room. "How did you sleep last night?" I asked.

"Not well. I had too much on my mind."

"I half-expected a knock at my door," I said, surprised at letting my true desire slip out.

"Are you kidding me?"

"Well, no. I mean, yes." I had such mixed emotions. I didn't want him to get the wrong impression, or maybe I did.

"I won't make that mistake again," he said with a confident wink.

We spent a tiring fourteen hours in that workshop. Each time Bob answered a question or made a comment, I wondered if he was sending me subtle messages. I could feel him looking at me when I was speaking. I had a hard time concentrating on the workshop.

I sat alone in my room afterwards wondering if he would be

true to the promise he made that morning. He tapped on my door around midnight. I opened it and welcomed a new chapter of my life.

The days and weeks that followed were manic. We stole moments together every chance we could through furtive telephone calls and emails. For Bob's next visit to Toronto, we planned a twenty-four-hour escape from the city, our work, our lives and everyone who knew us.

Snow fell softly as we drove up a country road into the horseshoe driveway at a nineteenth-century inn. The red-bricked hotel was reminiscent of a southern manor with its large white columns and its windows armed with black shutters. A solarium jutted out from the south end, offering a view of the vast wooded property. White lights twinkled on the garland everywhere for the holidays.

I felt like I was stepping into another era as we entered the inn. The charm of the place made it a perfect getaway from the ordinariness of our lives. That evening we enjoyed a gourmet dinner before returning to our suite. A large fireplace, mahogany furniture, white linens, an overstuffed down comforter and pillows, and a bathtub for two surrounded us in luxury. What I welcomed most was us being able to spend an extended period of time alone together.

We lit a fire and snuggled into each other's arms in front of the warm flames. Before long our passion consumed us. Our lovemaking took me beyond my body and mind to a place I had never been. My consciousness expanded, filling the room in a surreal way, as if I was floating. I felt safe, at peace, at home.

"I love you," Bob whispered. "I'm not sure how this is possible, but I think I've always loved you."

I hugged him. "I love you, too." The expansive truth of my words reverberated through my entire being.

We cuddled and playfully discussed an imaginary future together. In our reverie, we saw ourselves in the years to come returning to this inn — our special place.

"I can see us sitting in the solarium, surrounded by gardens in the summertime, eating cucumber sandwiches and sipping iced tea," Bob said.

"Yes, but egg salad sandwiches. I hate cucumbers!"

"Okay," he laughed. "I see us wandering the property, like one of those old couples who still hold hands and enjoy each other's company after years together."

I smiled. I clearly saw myself growing old with Bob, even after our short time together — something I never imagined with any of the other men who had been in my life.

"This time I see George and Martha as truly happy," Bob said, referring to the couple he playfully invented after our first kiss.

CHAPTER 4

Bad Timing

After driving Bob to the airport, I returned with reluctance to the apartment I shared with David. It was the Friday before Christmas and his MBA class was having a party. I couldn't muster the energy to join him. He wasn't pleased but he went without me.

I sat in the apartment's stillness and reflected upon my respective relationships with Bob and David. I felt like a hermit crab that had outgrown her shell. My home, my partner, my life no longer fit me. It was scary to think about leaving and starting a new life. While I felt alone and vulnerable, my heart was clear: I had fallen in love with Bob. What I felt was so much greater than a mere infatuation. It was like a deep remembering that went beyond my logical mind – a peacefulness that comes from being truly cherished.

It seemed crazy but I felt without a doubt only a few weeks after our first kiss that I wanted to spend the rest of my life with Bob, if given the chance. I doubted I would get that opportunity. There were so many obstacles standing between us. He was married with children, and thirteen years my senior. Living in different cities and yet working for the same company further complicated things. The safer route would have been to stay with David, but I had learned a valuable lesson years earlier when I'd felt a similar tug-of-war between my heart and my head.

Back in my MBA school days, I made a great connection with a guy shortly after breaking up with a long-time boyfriend. As soon as my old boyfriend learned about my new relationship, he tried to get back together with me. My head kept saying I should give the long-term relationship another chance, but my heart leaned towards a man I hardly knew. This internal battle raged for months as I vacillated between the relationships. In the end, both relationships fizzled as a result of my indecision.

I didn't want to make that kind of mistake again. Neither would I silence my heart for a safe bet. I knew I had to leave David, whether or not I had a shot with Bob.

The next morning I told David that I was leaving. He tried to persuade me to stay, but my mind was made up. I felt terrible hurting him, but I knew it would be worse dragging things out. A few weeks after my departure, David began dating a woman from his class. Our breakup was probably the best thing for him, as he went on to marry this new love and have children with her. My journey with Bob wouldn't be as straightforward.

After I left David, I became preoccupied with finding another place in Toronto to live and store my stuff. Bob and I remained in frequent contact by phone and email. We also occasionally saw each other. My friends and family were upset with me for throwing away a five-year relationship for a married man I hardly knew. I had to admit my choices didn't seem the wisest.

Bob faced his own challenges. "I can't concentrate," he said. "All I can think about is you and our time together. This isn't fair to my wife, but I don't know what to do. I want to be with you so badly, but I have a commitment to her and to the kids."

He didn't want his children to endure a divorce. He didn't feel he deserved to be happy at their expense. All of his life he had done what others had expected of him. He'd lost touch with who he was and what really mattered to him. He didn't like the man he had become, especially with his children: short-tempered, judgmental and emotionally distant.

Bob's internal battle went on for weeks until he finally decided to tell his wife the truth. She was devastated. She had no idea how unhappy he'd been. Instead of kicking him out, she asked him to try to work things out for the sake of their marriage and children. He was surprised by her level-headed response. It only added to his guilt. Placing her in such awkward circumstances made him feel terrible.

"This is the call you've been dreading," he said to me on the phone. "I can't see you anymore. My wife has asked me to give our marriage a second chance. It's the least I can do."

I froze. *This can't be happening.* My throat constricted and my stomach knotted as my fear of his leaving me became reality. I knew from my experience about that allure of a second chance at a relationship, and how it rarely worked out. I begged him not to go through with his decision. He understood my upset but was resigned to do the right thing. I could tell by his quiet measured tone that it was terribly difficult for him.

"Please understand. This is something I need to do. I am so sorry. I hate that I'm hurting you. I know you'd never do that to me. If only we had met under different circumstances, at a different time in our lives. Maybe one day..." His voice trailed off. "Well, it's just bad timing. I'm sorry."

I hung up the phone, shattered. *Is it possible that I will never hear from him again, never see his face, never feel his arms around me, never feel such love?* The room spun. I wanted to throw up. I always knew our relationship might end this way, but now that it had, I was in shock.

I dressed and went to work in a mental fog. *How am I going to get through this?* I had never felt such helplessness. My black-and-white world had returned. After experiencing such color, I didn't know how I would spend the rest of my life in shades of gray.

He sent an email later that same day. "Lee, I'm so sorry. I am trying to get through the day. I have to tell you that my heart is totally broken for what I have done to the person I love the most in the world."

My heart leaped. *He's feeling as devastated as I am! Maybe there's still hope? He just needs time. He won't be able to deny his heart. I can help him through this.*

The next few months were the hardest I experienced in my life up to that point. I wasn't able to let him go. I risked my own peace of mind and dignity by staying in touch with him. I believed that our love could see us through anything, including this. My illusion that all would eventually work out was fed by him remaining in contact through company email. "I just have to let you know that you are totally on my mind always," he wrote. "My heart aches horribly. There are no words to express my feelings."

Email was still relatively new in those days and we only had access through the server at work. When I arrived home at night, I was disconnected from Bob who couldn't phone while he was at home. I watched TV, read self-help books, went out with friends, anything to distract myself from the weight of my thoughts.

After several months, I grew tired of the heartbreak and loneliness. So when an opportunity arose to take a job in California as a marketing director for a global wine company, I jumped at it. I knew accepting the position would mean the end of any chance I had with Bob, but I felt I had to move forward with my life.

When Bob learned of my plans to leave Canada, he reached out to me. He expressed his fear of losing me forever and suggested that we give our relationship another try. After days of internal debate, I decided to turn down the unique career opportunity in favor of giving Bob another chance.

Bob and his wife officially separated. He rented a Montreal apartment. We began seeing each other every weekend, alternating between cities. This time our relationship was out in the open. It was a relief to be able to express our love for each other openly with our families and colleagues. Bob introduced me to his children. Our new life together began to feel almost normal. Within a couple months, we celebrated our first Christmas together. It was also the first time Bob spent the holidays without his children, who were with their mother. The nostalgia of the time of year reminded us how far we'd come since our country getaway the prior Christmas. It also brought up unsettled feelings in Bob. He missed his children and felt bad about not being with them. Early in January, he once again called me in turmoil. "I don't feel I truly gave my marriage and family a fair chance. I rushed things because I feared losing you. For their sake, I need to give my marriage another try. I need to sacrifice what I really want for their happiness."

"No, not again! We've come so far." I'd given so much — the chance at a great job opportunity, along with time, energy and so much love — all to make our relationship work, and here he was tossing it all away again. I knew there wasn't much hope in changing his mind, but I felt I had to try. We agreed to meet in Toronto one last time to say goodbye. I did everything I could to convince him to reconsider, but he was committed to his decision. I felt the weekend slip away like the sand in an hourglass. We stood outside my apartment on an unseasonably warm Sunday afternoon, clinging to each other. *This time he's not coming back. It's really over.*

"I'll always love you," he said, looking at me with tears streaming down his face. "I wish things could've been different for us. I know that to my dying day I will think of you. There will always be a part of me that will be with you." He held me close, kissed me on the lips and left for his car. I watched as he drove away down my tree-lined street. I felt my heart break as his car turned the corner and fell out of sight. *He's gone and he's not coming back.* I felt utterly alone.

I spent the evening crying. The next morning at work I received an email from him. "I miss you. I spent the drive home thinking about you. I don't know how I'm going to do this." Another glimmer of hope...

After a year of repeated heartbreak, I was battle-scarred. My emotions were raw, confidence deflated and spark fading. I needed a fresh start. I left our company for a new opportunity at a large media organization. The steep learning curve of the new job was a welcomed distraction. I met a lot of new people my own age. Hope started to return. *Maybe I'll meet someone new here.* My passion for travel reignited my spark. I had put traveling on hold for the past year. Now I could explore the world again.

Bob stayed in his apartment, maintaining his independence as he tested the waters with his wife once again. After a couple of months, his resolve weakened and he phoned. "How are you?"

"I'm getting back on my feet," I told him, trying to muster more confidence than I felt. "I have a great new job and I'm going to Nepal and India." We had talked about traveling together, but never had the chance. He told me he was happy for me, but I could hear the regret in his voice.

"It's not working," he confessed. "I'm so unhappy." With those few words, I was back. All my efforts to move forward without him tossed aside. We began talking regularly. He hinted at how he would love to travel with me. We fantasized about what it would be like to escape to the other side of the world together. Finally, I asked him to join me. He jumped at the opportunity.

We started our trip in Kathmandu at the aptly named Shangri-La Hotel. It was a peaceful oasis for our reunion. The property offered Zen gardens, plunge pools, candle-lit paths at nightfall, and a spectacular mountain view. Each day we experienced a new adventure. We took a plane ride over Mount Everest, hiked through remote villages to watch the sunrise over the Himalayas, road on elephants into the jungle looking for tigers, and toured the world's greatest monument to love: the Taj Mahal. On the way home, we stopped in London for a whirlwind tour of the city. The whole trip was the most exciting and exotic that either of us had ever experienced. Despite this, I sensed he was still emotionally torn.

After three glorious weeks together, Bob and I returned to our separate homes and reality. The next morning, he phoned me to tell me that it had been the trip of a lifetime, but that he had missed his kids and regretted having been away from them for so long. He explained that throughout the trip he couldn't shake the feeling that no matter how much he wanted to be with me, he just couldn't do it. He was sorry.

Once again I was crushed. *Our connection through our adventures had strengthened our bond. Yet he's ready to throw it all away again!* By this point, I was furious. *How could he do this to me again, after all we've been through? This yo-yo relationship has been going on for a year and a half. I'm tired of being rejected.*

My anger propelled me. *I'm done! No more emails, telephone calls, no more contact whatsoever. This time I'm really moving on!*

The anger made it easier. Any time I thought of Bob, I reminded myself of the immense disappointments and painful heartache.

Troubles had erupted at my workplace by this point. The company had been bought by a renowned slash-and-burn media tycoon. There were rumors that my division would be closed. I was put on a project that had me commuting three hours daily. This gave me a lot of time to think about the previous eighteen months on and off with Bob. My life had been turned upside down waiting for him, hoping we could start a life together one day. I was beginning to gain the confidence that I could get on with life without him.

For the first time since I met Bob, I seriously contemplated dating again. Truth be told, I also wanted to get back at him. Being with another man felt like a good way to do it. I kept myself active with sports and socializing with large groups of friends in the hope of meeting someone. However, no one even remotely interested me. So I poured myself into my work.

A short time later, my division was shut down. I received a large separation package to compensate for having been hired away from a steady position. With renewed confidence and financial security, I had the time to look for an ideal new job. Within a couple of weeks, an international development organization asked me to lead its fundraising division. I saw this as an opportunity to channel my training and skills into something that would make a positive impact. The job would also permit me to travel the world, meet extraordinary people, all while further developing my expertise. This was a big step up for me, but I took it. Even though my love life was in the toilet, my career was rocking.

After several months without contact, Bob called me out of the blue. "How're you doing?" I wanted to leap with excitement, but I had worked so hard to get over him. "I'm doing fine," I responded with caution.

"I miss you." His words caused a familiar tug at my heart.

"I miss you, too," I said hesitantly.

"I've had a terrible time."

"Sorry to hear things aren't going well for you," I said flatly.

"I've given my marriage a good chance and nothing has changed. I'm completely miserable. We've decided to get a divorce. I don't expect that you will want me back at this point. I just wanted you to know."

Hope kindled in my heart, but I didn't want to rip open that wound again. "Well, that's good," I said. "At least now you have clarity."

"Yes, it's crystal clear but, in the process, I've messed up what we had," he said with regret.

"It's been tough, I'll give you that. I'm not ready to jump back into a relationship with you. But if you do move forward with the divorce and start to take concrete actions, there may be a chance for us," I said, giving him hope while remaining cautious.

Bob filed for divorce and began the long and difficult process of figuring out with his wife how to share time with their children and divide their assets. Soon after, I went on a month-long trip to West Africa for my new job. The time apart, connecting only through emails, allowed me to slowly rebuild my trust in Bob. While I was away, he found us an apartment in a quaint small town north of Montreal. Within a few months, his uncontested divorce was finalized. I could hardly believe that the difficult times were behind us. We were ready to finally build a life together.

We had decided that it would be best if I moved to the Montreal area so Bob could remain close to his children. However, both the real estate and job markets in Quebec were soft. It was too risky for me to leave my job in Toronto while all of Bob's money was still tied up in his family home, so we had to wait until it sold. For over two years we lived in a holding pattern between two cities, waiting for a buyer. When one finally came through, we made plans to get married.

Almost to the day four years after our romance began, we flew to Bali for our wedding. We had discussed many options for our nuptials. Bali's luscious beauty, esoteric and exotic vibe created a magical and romantic setting for a ceremony. My parents and two of our close friends joined us to see our exchange of vows. I could not have imagined a more perfect moment as I looked around me. We all stood in a pagoda decorated with lush flowers and Balinese batik overlooking the Indian Ocean as the sun neared the horizon at dusk. After the ceremony, Bob and I stood in silence, arm in arm watching the final rays of the sun disappear into the ocean. *We are finally here! I can't believe it. We are going to spend the rest of our lives together, for better or worse, richer or poorer, in sickness and in health. Is this too good to be true?* Even in this moment of bliss, I feared the possibility of losing him again.

CHAPTER 5

What a Wonderful World

I loved my new life with Bob. Spending every single evening together and waking up next to him each morning were gifts I had waited so long to enjoy. Nevertheless, there were some major adjustments to be made. For the first few months I spent my days in a high-school classroom. The dreary walls, florescent lighting and constant drone of the heating system didn't exactly inspire learning. My classmates were teenagers and recent immigrants who, like me, needed to improve their French to get ahead in our predominantly francophone province. I'd grown up in Montreal and studied French in school, but lost any proficiency I once had after living in Toronto for eighteen years. It was humbling to be jobless and back in a high-school setting to take French classes for a second time. I tried to convince myself that this was an opportunity for a fresh start. The allure of more freedom and flexibility in my work and in my life made me consider starting my own business. I wasn't concerned that I wasn't fluent enough in French or that I didn't have any market contacts in Quebec. I figured my experience was more than enough to attract business. I developed a local network of clients and collaborators and my business slowly grew.

Bob and I discussed having a child. Being in his late forties, he was apprehensive about raising a baby again. He was also concerned about how people would judge him, especially given that fatherhood later in life was not very common in those days. Despite these reservations, we decided to start a family and I became pregnant within a few months. I was ecstatic. Bob was happy, but holding his breath a little, knowing what I was about to learn: how all-consuming child-rearing is.

A massive snowstorm in early April heralded our son's birth. A week later, we celebrated Bob's fiftieth birthday by taking Kaiden home from the hospital. My first year as a mother was transformative for me and for our relationship. I couldn't believe how fiercely I could love my son. I looked at Kaiden for long periods of time, just watching his every movement and feeling as if my heart would burst out of my chest with joy. I shared my feelings with Bob. He already knew how it felt, as this was his fourth time around. I began to better appreciate the emotional turmoil he felt during the early days of our relationship when he struggled to stay in an unhappy marriage for the sake of his children.

The physical and emotional demands of motherhood were much greater than I had anticipated. The lack of sleep, the constant focus on keeping another human being alive were much harder than anything I'd ever done. Our relationship also felt the stress as we continually shelved our own needs for the constant demands of parenthood. Differing points of view on how to take care of and raise our child added further friction. This tension was far more menacing than the challenges we had faced up until that point.

Before Kaiden's first birthday, Bob's company was bought out and his position made redundant. He was offered a severance package for his twenty-one years of service. For the first time in his adult life he was unemployed. It was a terrible blow to his self-esteem. He was tempted to bank the severance package and focus on finding new work, but we recognized that this was a unique opportunity that might not come around again. We needed to rekindle our relationship and to take some time to bond as a family. So we decided we would take a six-week adventure through France and Spain.

As we planned our trip, I could see Bob's enthusiasm and confidence return. Excitement and energy refueled our relationship, too. Just prior to the trip, I became pregnant. We were delighted and a little bit scared – traveling with a baby, another one on the way, and no foreseeable income. However, our trip brought us back to ourselves and to each other. The time we spent overseas was filled with precious moments: playing in a park in view of the Eiffel Tower, splashing in the Mediterranean, strolling through medieval villages in Provence and castles in the Loire Valley, touring vineyards and enjoying candlelit dinners while Kaiden slept in his stroller. The most memorable occasion was Kaiden taking his first steps on Spanish soil.

Our trip had its difficult moments as well. While I celebrated my second Mother's Day, I lost the baby I was carrying. Though it was early in the pregnancy, I was devastated. I wanted so much to have another child and a sibling for Kaiden.

When we returned home, we continued the leisurely lifestyle that we had adopted in Europe, spending time in local parks and cafés. We took another trip to western Canada with Bob's son Kevin, who was fourteen at the time, to visit our families. We bonded as we drove to the rugged west coast of Vancouver Island in an overstuffed hippy touring van. Bob played his guitar while he sat next to Kevin in the back row of seats. Kaiden and I sang along from the middle row, as my parents enjoyed the concert from the front. After leaving my parents, we stopped in Calgary on the way home to spend time with Bob's brothers and to visit the Rockies. I hadn't been back since I lived there in my early twenties for a year after finishing my undergraduate degree. It was fun to show Bob all of my old stomping grounds. My fondest memory was when Kaiden mooed the first time he saw a large elk crossing the road in front of our car thinking it was a cow.

We thoroughly enjoyed the five months of adventures since Bob had left his job, but knew we had to return to reality and start looking for work. On a September morning, before jumping back on the productivity treadmill, we took an early stroll to a park. The sun was shining brightly, promising a late-summer day ahead, but the morning's serenity was disrupted by three Canadian fighter jets overhead from a nearby Air Force base. We both acknowledged how strange their flight was and then shrugged it off. When we returned home, I received a call from my sister telling me to turn on the TV. I switched on the news as the second plane crashed into the Twin Towers. In a heartbeat our blissful bubble was shattered. For the rest of the day, we sat glued to the TV, while our toddler played with his toys oblivious to the chaos that was unfolding around the world. His serene reality would remain intact for a little longer, thank goodness.

In the weeks that followed 9/11, I felt a strong urge to take action to make a difference with my life. At the same time, I wanted to cocoon. In the face of so much death, I was reminded of the importance of love and of living in the moment. It was during this time that I became pregnant again. I wanted this baby more than ever, especially after losing one a few months earlier. Yet having another child while neither of us was working also made us nervous. I delved into my heart and the natural rhythm of my body to quell my fears. I began looking for clients while this new life was growing inside me.

Bob searched for a job. His severance helped to sustain us for several more months, and we were rewarded for our patience and trust in the Universe. In early July 2002, I gave birth to a healthy and gorgeous baby boy. We named him Kerrsen. The very next day, Bob received two job offers. He chose the more stable opportunity, working as the sales director for a large packaged goods company. It was time for us to play it safe for a while. Life started to fall back into a routine. We were both busy and happy. I was preoccupied with the baby, and Bob was eager to start his new job. It wasn't long, however, before our peaceful lives were turned upside down again.

The following winter, Bob's health began to decline. His persistent cough turned into pneumonia. One doctor noticed that his thyroid was swollen. Further investigation indicated that he needed surgery to remove it. There was a chance that he might have thyroid cancer. A couple of weeks later, he went into the hospital for day surgery. I sat alone in the waiting room during his operation, afraid of losing him. I had a baby, a toddler, and a husband who might have cancer. I was in a city that still didn't feel like home with no family and only a few friends. The surgery went a lot longer than expected. I began to panic. I imagined the worst. I checked each person being wheeled into the recovery room hoping to see Bob. Finally, four hours later, Bob arrived. The doctor told us that Bob's thyroid had become the size of a baseball and had to be removed, but he would be fine with medication. I almost collapsed in Bob's hospital bed with relief.

The months following Bob's surgery were difficult. He tired easily and frequently became sick. He had to make regular visits to the doctor and other specialists to determine the right balance of medication. His health gradually improved, but he never regained his prior energy, which made his new job all the more challenging. When things returned close to normal, we discussed giving up our rented apartment and moving to a home in the country. Bob's kids were getting older and more independent, which meant we didn't have to remain in the city for them. A rural community west of Montreal attracted us. The picturesque town on the banks of the Ottawa River had expansive wooded properties with sprawling perennial gardens — a utopian place to raise children. We were so excited to buy our first house together and move to this idyllic setting.

As with other parts of our lives, the move did not go smoothly. Our landlord made it difficult for us to get out of our lease. Our upscale neighborhood had seemed safe until a drug dealer moved into the apartment building's basement. After a shooting right outside involving the tenant and the Russian mafia, we were more determined than ever to get out of the area. We pleaded and negotiated with the landlord until he begrudgingly let us out of our lease.

As we packed our belongings to move within a few days, Bob received a phone call.

"I think I'm about to be fired," he said afterwards.

"Why? What happened?"

"I just found out that my boss is on his way to Montreal from Toronto to meet with me, but he won't tell me what it's about."

My heart sank. *Not again! Not as we are about to leap into a large mortgage!* I pleaded with the Universe.

Bob's hunch was right. He was let go as part of a company downsizing for the second time in three years. The job loss devastated him. In his mid-fifties, his prospects of finding another position looked grim. Corporate life had worn thin on him as well. I had been working part time, but my income was not enough to carry us. When movers arrived to pick up our belongings on the following Monday, we discovered that the company we had hired to move us had gone bankrupt. The people at our door were from the company that had bought out the other movers less than 24 hours earlier. I couldn't believe it. Our life seemed to be spiraling downwards.

"Should we trust these people with our stuff?" Bob asked.

"Do you think it's a sign? Maybe we aren't meant to move. Well, I think it's too late to do anything now. We'll have to find a way to make it work. We always do."

"Could things get worse?" Bob asked dejected.

It was the end of February and minus forty degrees Fahrenheit outside — the coldest day of the year. As the movers carried the furniture into our new place, our toddlers ran around the frigid house. The day seemed to take forever as I tried to keep the house warm and the children out of trouble. Near midnight, the moving truck finally drove away. With the boys asleep, Bob and I sat down at last in our new house surrounded by boxes piled to the ceiling. We opened a bottle of wine and relaxed into the perfect silence of our country home. When we woke up the next morning, there were three deer in our backyard. I believe they were there to welcome us. The connection to nature that I immediately felt in our new home gave me a deep sense of peace. I knew on some level that I was where I was meant to be. We didn't know how we would pay the mortgage, but we knew we had arrived home.

Instead of job hunting again, Bob wanted to try being an entrepreneur. He opened a small food brokerage firm but the market was fiercely competitive at the time and the business never took off. We decided that the best prospects for our household's income would be for me to focus on expanding my business, with Bob's help. He would also take over the full-time care of the kids. It took me a lot of time and energy to drum up business, but contracts eventually started to roll my way. Our role reversal was a difficult adjustment. I longed to spend more time with our young boys, while Bob was plagued with guilt for not contributing to the family income. Yet he flourished as a stay-at-home dad. He did a great job nurturing the boys and looking after the household. He also moved his ninety-year-old mother to a local seniors' residence so he could look after her better.

As we quickly became enchanted with our new community, Bob also became interested in getting involved with the municipality's administration. "What would you think if I ran for town council?" he asked one day.

"You would be perfect for the job!" I welcomed the notion of him using his unique talents and expertise in a way that would give him a sense of joyful fulfilment.

"I would like to find a way to give back, to use my business experience in a positive way," he explained.

"It will also be a great way to expand our social network," I added.

He worked hard, knocking on doors to get known. I was so proud of him as I watched him win over people with his authentic charm. He was deemed the underdog as a newcomer to the town, yet won with an overwhelming majority of votes.

Bob rose to this new challenge, throwing himself into all sorts of committees and projects, which restored his self-confidence. Our life in the community steadily expanded with his new role as a councilor, the boys' school activities, and family obligations. Our life together was full but stable. Our contentment did not last for long.

A year later, my father was diagnosed with bladder cancer. His battle was surprisingly short. I said goodbye to him for the last time within months of his diagnosis. His demise was the first time I experienced someone so close to me dying. I was torn between my concern for my mother who had just lost the love of her life – her soulmate – and my own intense grief. I could not accept the finality – the idea that I would never have contact with my father again. So, I set out to learn more about how I might connect spiritually with him. This was the first crack in my awakening. The next crack arrived with the force of a sledgehammer.

Part 2

"*Your pain is the breaking of the shell that encloses your understanding. Even as the stone of the fruit must break, that its heart may stand in the sun, so must you know pain.*"

– Kahlil Gibran

CHAPTER 6
Hold On

Gunner, an adorable nine-month-old Labrador Retriever and Husky mix, was the latest addition to our family. With two boys, two cats and a dog, our family felt complete. Bob and I were happy. Our life together flowed easily. We felt tremendously fortunate.

We marveled at how our sons, who had the same parents, could be so different. Kerrsen, the younger one who had plump cheeks with deep dimples and curly blonde hair, was gregariously happy-go-lucky. Kaiden, who had more slender features, straight black hair, freckles and Bob's cleft chin, was introverted and serious. Kerrsen did well in a traditional school setting, following the curriculum and quickly catching onto concepts. Kaiden excelled in a more self-directed learning environment. One family trait they both shared was a devilish twinkle in their azure-blue eyes.

They were five and seven years old when we received the cancer diagnosis. Despite their young age, they were acutely aware of cancer. Their school had made them aware of it. We weren't sure how to tell them about Bob's illness. Our instincts as parents were to hold back the truth to protect them from the pain. Yet we knew we couldn't shelter them from the reality for very long. They would sense that something was wrong. Plus news spread fast in our small town. We feared they would hear things at school. So we decided soon after receiving the diagnosis to hold a family meeting.

"Have we done something wrong?" Kaiden asked.

"No, honey, it's nothing like that. We have something to tell you." *Brace yourself because this is going to hurt like hell,* I thought, taking a deep breath. "I'm so sorry I have to tell you this." I paused. *Just say it, Lianne.* "Daddy has cancer."

"Is Daddy going to die?" Kerrsen asked.

Another crack in my heart as I tried to answer honestly this most difficult question without shattering their hope. "No one knows when someone's going to die," I said.

Bob stiffened and took a noticeable breath. "Daddy's very sick, but I am going to fight with everything I have to get better."

"Cancer is very hard to predict," I added. "You remember our friend Wendy? She fought cancer and survived. Poppa wasn't so lucky. What we can tell you is that Daddy's doctors are going to do everything they can to help him to get better. And we are going to let you know as we learn more. You can always ask us anything. Okay?"

"Daddy's NOT going to die! I just know it," Kaiden declared

matter-of-factly. His knotted eyebrows and pursed lips belied his certainty, but I felt a sense of relief when he said those words aloud. Hearing them helped me believe they could be true.

"That's right. Daddy's not going to die!" Kerrsen echoed his brother, bolstering his own courage.

If only all our wishful thinking had come true. Shortly after the diagnosis, Bob's health declined rapidly. It had been only a few weeks since his biopsy but the lining that surrounded his lung was again filling up with fluid and literally squeezing the breath out of him. He couldn't walk up a flight of stairs without being depleted of air. He was in a lot of pain around his upper back where he had been operated. I hardly recognized him — huddled over, thin, weak and struggling to breathe. This was not the strong man I'd fallen in love with. We knew we had to do something quickly, because he wouldn't survive long in this condition.

When we saw the oncology and radiology specialists, they recommended "debulking," which meant surgically removing the lung with the tumor and then blasting the left thoracic cavity with an aggressive round of chemotherapy and radiation. We needed to get a special PET scan first to see if the disease had spread beyond the cavity. If it had, the surgery would be pointless.

Dr. Mulder had told us on the phone that he believed the cancer was inoperable, but we knew that Bob's only hope of survival was surgery. We had to convince Dr. Mulder to do it. We went into his office armed with the PET scan results, determined to get his approval for the required procedure.

He reviewed the scan results, then looked up at us. "When I

started my career, my mentor used to tell people who had this type of cancer to take a bottle of scotch and a fishing rod and enjoy the little time they had left." *Where is he going with this glibness?* I wondered. "Today, we have some tools to fight it, but they are only marginally successful," he continued. "This kind of surgery is very difficult and dangerous. The recovery is long and painful, and the prognosis is not great." *Is he trying to scare us? If so, he is doing a good job.*

He finally shared that the operation would remove one of Bob's lungs and possibly part of his heart, ribs and diaphragm.

Bob's eyes welled up with tears and his voice cracked as he looked directly at the doctor. "I have a five- and a seven-year-old. I am not ready for scotch and a fishing rod. I want to fight this with everything I've got. What would you do, if it were you?" Bob tried to appeal to the doctor's sense of compassion.

Dr. Mulder didn't hesitate. "I would take a chance with the surgery."

"Then I would like the same chance. I would like to try the surgery." Bob's voice became steadier. I was impressed watching him negotiate in his weak state with the surgeon. He'd been a shrewd negotiator in his sales career. Now he was negotiating for his life.

"Okay, let's try it then." Mulder escorted us to the door. "You will have some pre-operation tests and we'll try to schedule you for the earliest available time."

As we walked out of the office, we were both relieved and terrified. Two weeks later we were notified that Bob's surgery was scheduled for the next day. *Holy crap! In less than 24 hours,*

Bob is going to have a potentially life-threatening procedure. I was relieved that we wouldn't have to wait, but afraid he might have complications from the surgery or, worse, not make it through.

The next morning, as Bob was being wheeled into surgery, I said: "You know, if anything happens to you–"

"I thought we were going to stay positive," Bob said.

"I am, but I have to say this anyway: If anything happens to you, I'll be okay... I'll do my best to take care of the boys, the way you would want me to do. And I know you'll be with me in spirit throughout..."

"I know. I trust you completely," he reassured me.

The waiting room was packed with our family members and close friends. We sat together for hours waiting for news. Coincidently, our friend's daughter was a medical student on the surgical ward that day. She kept popping into the operating room to get updates. "He's stable," she reported back. This helped to relieve the stress we were all feeling. After ten hours in surgery, a haggard Dr. Mulder entered the waiting room.

I held my breath.

"He's okay."

I let out a sigh of relief.

"We had a difficult time getting all the cancer, but we did our best." Then came the words I dreaded. "It looks like the cancer has spread to his lymph nodes. We removed a few nodes, which will be tested. If the cancer has spread into the lymphatic system, our chances of containing the cancer are less optimistic."

There was Dr. Doomsayer again. I'm not going to listen to him any more right now.

"Either way, he'll need chemotherapy and radiation to try to get any cancer cells that we weren't able to reach with the surgery," he added.

When he left, everyone gathered into a hug. "Let's not worry about the lymph nodes right now. Let's just focus on the fact that he's okay," I said more for myself than for anyone else.

As Bob regained consciousness in the Intensive Care Unit, he looked at the many tubes sprouting from his body to machines and said to his eldest daughter who was leaning over him, "I guess I don't look so good, eh?"

Tears welled up in my eyes as I saw signs of the old Bob coming back to life. *Maybe he is going to be okay,* I indulged myself in hopefulness.

Bob's recovery from the surgery was long and difficult, but he had a goal. He wanted to be home for Kaiden's eighth birthday. He focused on eating and resting enough to regain his strength and did the prescribed exercises to heal as quickly as possible. He likely pushed himself too hard in order to be released early, but it wasn't in time for Kaiden's birthday.

Soon after Bob's return home, I organized a belated party for Kaiden. I was impressed with Bob's stamina as he helped me host the party for a dozen eight-year-old boys and a magician. The following night we included Bob's older kids to celebrate their father's birthday as well. While nothing was said overtly, we all knew how special it was to be celebrating this birthday.

After everyone left and the boys were put to bed, Bob sat on the couch exhausted. He had only been out of the hospital for a couple of days. In all the commotion, we hadn't noticed that the tube earlier attached to his chest to drain fluid had fallen out. He had an appointment the next day to have the tube removed but, not wanting to take any chances, I called 911. The first responders arrived in minutes and took his vitals. Oddly enough, we met these same individuals earlier that day when they were putting out a small fire that had ignited in a sugar shack across the street from us. I found myself distracted by the coincidence that Bob had been kidding with these same guys only hours earlier and now they were assessing his medical condition.

I was also concerned about the boys and what they were overhearing. "Don't let them see me like this," Bob said, referring to the oxygen mask and heart monitor now placed on him. He was always concerned about the impact his illness might have on the boys. Kaiden had quietly come down the stairs when he heard the ambulance. He peeked around the corner to see what was happening. I quickly ushered him back upstairs.

"Is Daddy going to die?" There it was again, the dreaded question.

"I think he'll be okay. His tube came out and he has to go back to the hospital to get it checked," I tried to reassure him.

The first responders wheeled Bob out on a stretcher. I held the boys in my arms as we watched from the upstairs window. Bob waved and blew a kiss in the hopes of comforting them. I reassured them that he would be okay before I left them with a close friend to follow the ambulance.

Bob and I sat for hours in the overcrowded emergency room only to discover that he hadn't been in any danger after all. The attending emergency room physician patched up the wound where the tube had been disconnected and sent us on our way. This experience demonstrated to us how uncertain Bob's situation was. We would have to learn to deal with this reality.

In the months that followed Bob's recovery after his surgery, our primary focus was on managing his pain and getting him ready for what the doctors called the *tour de force*: chemotherapy and radiation treatment. We were keenly aware that the next stage of his treatment had to take place within twelve weeks of the surgery to be effective. Otherwise, any remaining cancer cells might regain ground. Bob's slow recovery had us worried that he wouldn't rebuild his strength in time.

We took a family vacation to Vermont to make the most of our time before Bob's next phase of treatment. It was so good to see Bob slowly taking up the activities he loved — playing with the kids, swimming, and even hiking. We arrived home from our getaway the night before the chemotherapy injections were scheduled to begin. We were anxious but eager to start. I unpacked our suitcases from the holiday and lay out the boys' costumes for the Carnival Day at camp the next morning. I marveled at the contrast within my family's life: hospitals and chemotherapy; vacations and camp.

After eight and a half hours of hospital miscommunications, including confusion over drug compatibility, and a lengthy chemotherapy session, we left the hospital with a bag full of pills and a load of instructions. As the chemo nurse said goodbye, she told us that we had one of the most complicated cases she had ever seen. It seemed to be the kind of luck that followed us. Other strange things began to happen soon after.

A few days later, while we were having dinner, Kaiden squealed, "There's a heron on the deck!" Sure enough, this normally shy creature was looking through a screened window at us from the deck's railing. We weren't sure whether it was some kind of sign or the bird had just been attracted by the smell of the tuna casserole we were eating. Herons were Bob's favorite bird. Earlier that same day, two herons had passed in front of Bob during his walk by a local wetland. Some native cultures believe that a heron sighting is good luck. As we began the *tour de force* chemo and radiation, I hoped Bob's encounter with three herons in a single day was a true sign of positive things to come.

The chemotherapy was really challenging for Bob. During each session, he spent most of a day hooked up to a potent chemical drip. Over the next three weeks he went through a roller coaster of physical hardships. First he became nauseous. Then he experienced days of extreme fatigue which he said was the worst side effect of all. It robbed nearly all of his life energy. Just as his body started returning back to life, he would go for another session and the pattern would begin all over again.

Bob always found a way to get through these difficult experiences. He never seemed to let them get the better of him. He jokingly described the radiation sessions as his time in the torture chamber. The muscles and nerves that connected his arm to his back were damaged during the operation, leaving him with a chronic firing and misfiring of the nerves. Holding his arm over his head for a couple of seconds, let alone minutes, was excruciating. It was sheer willpower that allowed him to last through the twenty-minute radiation sessions. Each time he was sure he would be unable to tolerate the pain. Gritting his teeth, he kept his hand over the call button. During the dozens of times Bob had to keep his arm overhead, he only had to stop midway through a treatment once.

By mid-October 2008, he had undergone five of the six prescribed chemotherapy sessions, as well as five weeks of daily radiation. The surgery and treatments had taken away all of his fight.

"I can't," he said before the final treatment was scheduled. "I don't want to do any more treatments. I've had enough."

I worried that veering from the prescribed medical path could hurt his potential recovery, but I suppressed my fear. "If you're sure, I trust you know what's best for you," I said.

A new PET scan was scheduled to determine whether the cancer cells had been eliminated. We felt it was time for another family trip to celebrate the end of Bob's treatment, as well as our tenth wedding anniversary. We wanted the trip to be something special for the kids so their memories wouldn't be only of hospitals and their father's illness. I was happy that we weren't going to receive the scan results until after the trip. As long as I didn't know the results, I could imagine the best possible scenario: the cancer eradicated, Bob becoming whole again, and our family getting back to normal. An all-inclusive stay in Jamaica was the perfect retreat. The boys and I went snorkeling, swimming and even spent time with stingrays and dolphins, while Bob watched and rested from the sidelines. Bob and I also found cherished moments to be alone together when the boys were occupied at the resort's Kids' Club. During one of those times, Bob held out a beautifully decorated box. "For you, on our anniversary," he said.

"But we had agreed that the trip was our gift to each other," I replied, surprised.

"I know, but I wanted to get you something to thank you for being by my side throughout everything, and to tell you how beautiful you are."

"I must be the luckiest woman alive!" I unwrapped the box to find a short silver necklace with a large round pendant that immediately reminded me of the circular wholeness of our love.

We came home to a cold November and the reality of the anticipated PET scan results. At the same time, the world had fallen into a financial crisis. As the United States pinned its hopes on a new president, we held onto the hope that we were through the worst of the cancer journey. I tried to quell my burning fear that we weren't and instead ride a wave of optimism for as long as possible. I prayed for the strength to handle whatever outcome presented itself. As we waited to be called into the doctor's office, we ran into an older couple we had met almost a year earlier when Bob went for his first biopsy. The other man had also gone for a biopsy and the results were not good. He sat there looking at us, obviously ill.

"I don't have much time," he told us.

Saddened, I looked into his wife's eyes with empathy. "I am so sorry," was all I could muster.

When we told them that we were there to get Bob's scan results, the wife smiled and said: "Good luck."

Oh God, how can she wish me luck when her life is falling apart?

I hope that if I find myself in the same situation I will have the same strength and grace.

A nurse ushered Bob and me into the doctor's small office. As we waited, we held hands and assured each other that no matter what the results, we would be okay. We had each other. Two doctors entered the room. We watched their every motion for clues. The first was the doctor who had told us months earlier to "debulk" the tumor. She was accompanied by Dr. Mulder, the surgeon who had done the "debulking." They both smiled and said to Bob: "Your test is clear!"

I couldn't understand at first what they were saying. "What do you mean?"

"There are no visible signs of the cancer," replied Dr. Mulder with guarded elation in his voice. This was the doctor who only months earlier said there was little to no hope. It seemed obvious that they were as surprised by the results as we were.

"This is a miracle!" Bob said.

"We still have to monitor you for signs of the cancer returning," replied Dr. Mulder.

He's always the downer.

"We will schedule you for another CAT scan in four months," he added.

"Yes, but this must be the best possible news we could have received, is it not?" asked Bob.

"Yes, it truly is," Dr. Mulder responded emphatically.

We walked out of that office elated. We could hardly believe our good fortune. The older couple was still in the waiting room. I could barely look at them. *How could we be so lucky when they were not?* She asked me about the results. I tried to downplay my enthusiasm. "There are no visible signs, but they have to continue to monitor his progress."

"Oh, that's good news," she smiled and patted her husband's leg. My heart ached for her. I said goodbye knowing I would probably never see her again. After spending so much time over the past year at the hospital, we were so happy that we wouldn't have to return for a few months.

We called Bob's family first, then my family and friends. Waves of exhausted relief rippled through our families and community. We took the boys out for a celebratory dinner at their favorite pizzeria to tell them our good news.

"Daddy doesn't have cancer anymore?" asked Kaiden.

"That's right, honey," I said.

"Great," he responded.

"Awesome," said Kerrsen.

They returned to their pizza, hardly skipping a beat. Bob and I were still trying to digest the news and here the kids were taking it as if it was no big deal.

We had been given a Christmas miracle. Even though the financial market was in turmoil and my consulting business collapsing with it, we were on top of the world. We wouldn't let ourselves believe that Bob was cured for good, but we did allow ourselves the hope that we had bought more time together.

CHAPTER 7

Have You Ever Seen the Rain?

I felt like a soldier returning from a tour of duty with post-traumatic stress disorder as I transitioned back into regular life. While the immediate dangers were gone, the year's traumatic events reverberated as aftershocks in my dreams and as unexpected panic attacks. Chronic stress was my new normal. I lived with the unrelenting fear of losing Bob, and the exhausting job of balancing everyone else's needs, but completely neglected my own. I was so fatigued that even after hours of sleep I still felt tired. I was tormented by the thought of being sent back into my personal war zone.

As I struggled to manage everything for our family, my business went into a tailspin. My consulting services were the first thing to be slashed by my clients during the economic uncertainty. It didn't help that I hadn't been as strongly focused on my business as usual while Bob underwent treatment. My sales dropped seventy-five percent from the previous year. I had survived one crisis only to be thrown into another. Lacking time and energy at that point to start anew, I decided to block out all financial worries. Each time fear bubbled up from my belly like burning lava, I did my best to change my thoughts. *Losing some money, even going bankrupt, is nothing compared to losing Bob. If he is healthy, I can get through anything.*

Bob was getting a little stronger each day, although he still tired easily and continued to experience intense pain where he had the surgery. Nevertheless, he returned to his work as a town councilor and gradually began resuming more responsibilities at home. I was thrilled to have my husband and best friend back. The boys were delighted to come home to their Dad every day.

With more time on my hands, I began reimagining what my work could ideally be. I craved more passion and meaning in my day-to-day work life. Social media was gaining popularity. Realizing these new communication avenues could help me to find a way to transform my work, I dove into the ins and outs of blogging, along with using Facebook, Twitter and other platforms to build my online presence and community. I began to imagine a new business for myself — one that had at its core the commitment to making a positive difference in the world. This helped me with my post-trauma-like symptoms. I felt on fire again. Bob and I had something new and positive to talk about. We were so fed up of the endless medical discussions. This gave us a way to reconnect with our shared passion for improving the world in some way, while supporting each other.

It felt so good for a change.

After my father had died two years earlier, a dear friend gave me the book *Conversations with God* by Neale Donald Walsch. It helped me to make sense of the first major loss in my life and rekindled my interest in my long-shelved personal spirituality. A year later, while Bob underwent treatment, I was introduced to other transformative books. I established a spiritual book club with some of the women I already knew as a way for me to further explore concepts and gain some community support. These gatherings nourished me. Our conversations pushed the boundaries of my beliefs and made me feel whole again. I was putting cancer on the back burner of my life, rather than have it define everything. I made dozens of new connections as word spread quickly about our spiritual book club. I had found my tribe. I remember thinking after one of these gatherings that I wished I could feel as inspired and full of life every day as I did after one of our meetings. I later would learn to be careful about what I wished for.

I took the boys for their last ski lesson on a sunny first day of March. The promise of spring in the air encouraged me to believe that the worst of the winter and our family's struggles were behind us. February is the month known for love. Yet for me it had been full of heartbreak over the past several years. Bob was diagnosed with terminal cancer the previous February. A year earlier, my father had died. And prior to that, Bob had lost his job in February. As I waited for the boys' lessons to end, it occurred to me that I had made it through this February unscathed.

As soon as we returned from the ski hill, I received a call that turned March into my new least favorite month. John, the husband of my dear friend, Heather, had died in a snowboarding accident. She had been among the close circle of friends helping me to deal with Bob's illness. I couldn't believe that her husband was suddenly gone, and in such an unexpected way. I rushed to Toronto to be by her side.

While I tried to focus on helping Heather and her two daughters, I kept imagining myself in her shoes. Our lives had been intertwined for so long. Our mothers went to school together and our large Catholic families were close. We both lived in Montreal as kids and then moved to Toronto at the same time, eventually going away to the same university. We both had strong, charismatic and outspoken husbands whom we loved tremendously. I tried unsuccessfully to brush off the feeling that her life was foreshadowing my own. I sensed that Bob felt this way, too, especially when her late husband's brothers played guitar and sang at his funeral.

I returned home with a heavy heart. I tried to shake off my dark mood as I accompanied Bob to an appointment to receive his latest CT scan results. We were optimistic, having received the news that he was cancer free only three months earlier. Everything would still be all right, we reassured ourselves. So, unlike the previous time, I didn't prepare myself properly for bad news.

Bob's radiologist was somber when she told us there were new spots on his remaining lung, as well as in his abdomen. We didn't fully understand the implications of these results. The oncologist delivered the second blow when she told us that there weren't any other reliable options for Bob. She left us with a mere glimmer of hope: a new trial therapy that was slated to begin at the hospital shortly. She suggested that Bob could be the first person in the trial chemotherapy.

While we waited for the new trial drug to crawl through the bureaucratic process, our hope of a cure began to fade. We were forced into a dangerous game of chicken. Bob could try an approved chemotherapy, but its success was unlikely. If he took that route, he would be disqualified from the trial chemotherapy. Yet waiting for the trial to start risked allowing the cancer to spread. To make matters worse, he only had fifty-percent odds of receiving the real trial drug therapy, instead of a placebo.

We tried to speed up Bob's access to the trial with calls to the hospital's ombudsman. We also encouraged Bob's oncologist to call the pharmaceutical company's headquarters in California. That finally worked. Bob was scheduled to start his first round of what we hoped was the trial chemotherapy. It was a strange time. A year earlier, Bob had been so terribly sick with chemotherapy that he would probably have done anything to avoid feeling like that again. Yet, hoping he wasn't being given the placebo, he now eagerly looked for side effects.

A few weeks into the trial, the doctor ordered another CT scan to determine Bob's progress. The results were mixed. His cancer had shrunk in some places and grown in others. As we started to leave the doctor's office in a discouraged state, she urged Bob to obtain pain advice from the hospital's palliative care unit. The word *palliative* formed a lump of anxiety in my stomach. Bob was reassured that this was only to help him with his pain, not to make end-of-life arrangements. It still felt like the beginning of the end.

We decided to take a family trip before Bob's health deteriorated further. There was a good chance that this would be our last trip together. We wanted it to be special, one that the boys and I would always remember. Disney World was the obvious choice with the boys aged six and eight. Bob, Kaiden and I all celebrated birthdays while on this trip. Knowing that these could be our last birthday celebrations all together was the ultimate test of our mental fortitude. I tried to remain present and enjoy myself while knowing the suffering that lay ahead for Bob, for all of us... and longing for a future of holidays and birthday celebrations that I sensed would never come to be.

On the night of Bob's fifty-ninth birthday, we celebrated at a chic California-style bistro in Orlando. The food and service were good, but not extraordinary. I felt they should have been, for his last birthday party. I almost wanted to tell the server about our situation, but stopped myself. *What could he possibly do to make this night better, even if he knew the circumstances?*

We spent most of the dinner in quiet contemplation, exhausted from the day at Disney. Fear got the better of me when I leaned over and whispered in Bob's ear, "I don't know how I'm going to do it without you. Up until this point, the boys have spent their whole lives with you and yet they will likely spend the rest of their childhood and entire adult lives without you." I glanced at Kaiden and Kerrsen, imagining them alone with me at sixteen and eighteen.

"I'm not leaving you." He sounded a bit hurt. I thought he meant that it wasn't his choice, but later I wondered if he meant he would always be with us in spirit to help guide the boys and me through the difficult times.

A couple of months later, I wanted to do something special for Father's Day. I tried to lift Bob's spirits by demonstrating the abundance of love for him. I asked our families and close friends to send pictures with an encouraging quote or a few words of their own, all of which I assembled into a special book for him. Some of Bob's family resisted my idea, concerned that Bob would take this gesture as an early eulogy. The matter turned into a family drama at a time when we needed to pull together. I finally had to ask Bob to say something to end the dispute. I realized that soon I wouldn't have him around to fight my battles for me. When Bob opened his gift, he was moved to tears. He soaked in the love and support that were expressed in each picture and every word. Over the weeks that followed, I noticed him on many occasions taking out the book and sitting with it quietly.

His daughter Kim's wedding was the high point of the summer and our last family celebration all together. Bob desperately wanted to make it through this special day without having to leave to lie down somewhere as he did during the course of a normal day. The combination of painkillers, a couple of drinks, and natural father-of-the-bride adrenaline kept him going.

The wedding day was the first time that Bob saw his former wife's family since their divorce, which definitely caused some unspoken tension at first. It quickly dissipated as Bob stoically accompanied his daughter down the aisle. As he presented Kim to her about-to-be husband, I sensed he was thinking, you'd better take care of my princess for me when I'm no longer here.

We sat in front of his former in-laws at the church. After the ceremony, I put out my hand to shake theirs. They responded stiffly. When I introduced them to my boys, they softened. Throughout the evening, I felt like an outsider. I stepped back, allowing Bob to have his time with his children, his earlier family and old acquaintances. At one point, Bob and I finally had a chance to dance. As I laced my arms around his neck, he pulled me closer. The dance of our bodies together was so familiar. As his torso pressed against me, I could feel my heart aching. *This could be our last dance.* I looked over his shoulder at the people on the crowded dance floor. I felt jealous of the other couples. *They don't know how lucky they are to have time, to have many more dances together.* Bob was my only connection to them. The next time I saw them would likely be at his funeral. I expected they would disappear from my life afterwards.

After the wedding, Bob's health declined rapidly. It was as if he had been remaining strong for his daughter. Once her special day was over, the pain and stress of his disease caught up with him. On top of everything, he had to emotionally deal with his mother moving to Calgary so two of his brothers could look after her. Over the past two decades, Bob primarily looked after her care as the only son who remained in the Montreal area. This forged a strong bond between them that was about to be ripped apart. It was excruciating to witness. Bob's mom wanted to stay close to her dying son. Leaving him would haunt her for years to come. I sensed Bob felt remorseful that he could no longer look after his mother. Even though they didn't say what they were thinking, I could sense they both knew that they might never see each other again.

Bob and I had to come to terms with the reality that he likely didn't have a lot more time. *Will we have one more anniversary together? One more Christmas?* I hoped, but there was no guarantee. We had to decide when and how we would best prepare the boys for the inevitable. We planned to tell them the truth, but we still wanted to protect them for as long as possible. We found an expert in children's bereavement. Carol Jonas made us understand that it was essential to tell the boys sooner rather than later. She also worked with them using art therapy and other methods to help them comprehend what was happening and express their feelings. After one of the sessions, Kerrsen arrived home with a gift for me: a white and pink fabric carnation attached to a pen with masking tape. As he handed it to me, he smiled and said: "You can spray Daddy's aftershave onto it so you will remember him when he dies." I was amazed by his thoughtfulness, especially at a time where he was undoubtedly worried about the near future and already suffering with the knowledge he would lose his father.

Kaiden was processing everything. "Mommy, when the palliative care house is finished, Dad can go there," he said to me casually one day in reference to the residence being constructed at the end of our block. "That way, we can visit him, and you can still look after us." I was moved yet saddened that he was having to sort out such heavy thoughts and emotions at such a young age. My heart broke for both of our sons.

It was autumn and the kids were returning to school. I often felt overwhelmed with the change in the family's schedules, the increasing demands of Bob's care, and my efforts to still try to keep my business afloat. Walking in the woods always helped me to clear my head. During one of my ritual morning walks, I stood among a circle of four pine trees – my favorite place on the path near our home. I felt a surge of energy as I belted out my distraught feelings. "What am I going to do? How am I going to survive this?" It was as if I was asking these sage pillars of life for advice. To my surprise, I heard a quiet but clear voice in my head say one simple word: plan. *Is that my imagination?* I wasn't sure. *What does that mean, plan?* Immediately I heard a response to my question in the same voice: make your lists, ask for help, organize yourself. It will help you to get through.

I was surprised by the clarity of the guidance. I figured it couldn't hurt to try to follow this advice. When I returned home, I solicited help from family members and friends, and made plans for the kids, my work and Bob's care. This eased the stress tremendously. The next week, I decided to return to my tree council for more wisdom. "What should I do now?" This time I heard the word: love. I was surprised again with the clarity and simplicity of the message. This time I knew intuitively the meaning behind the word. I was to spend as much time as I could with Bob. This turned out to be the best advice I could have ever received. It helped me to finally let go of my work and focus on Bob and the boys. I felt completely present in each moment for the first time in longer than I could remember.

The next week I asked my tree council for another message.

This time the answer scared me: brace yourself. *What the heck? What do I do with this message?* I heard the answer immediately: By doing what you have done for the past two weeks — preparing, taking care of yourself, and enjoying the beauty of the moment — you will weather the storm.

I imagined myself battening down the hatches as one does before an impending hurricane. This would be a Category 5, I was sure of it. Within days, I would rely on this sage advice to get through the most difficult experience of my life.

CHAPTER 8

Evie (I'm Losing You)

On the advice of Bob's oncologist, we reluctantly visited the hospital's palliative care unit to obtain pain management advice. With Bob's pain so severe and resistant to several medications, the medical staff offered him the most aggressive drug available: methadone. He was assured that it was effective and safe. While there, the attending physician urged Bob to sign a Do Not Resuscitate (DNR) form. We were uncomfortable taking this step as it felt like the beginning of the end, but we were told it was standard procedure. The doctor explained that a DNR was only for extreme circumstances when it would be better to let a person die naturally than attempt painful procedures to prolong life. Against our instincts, we signed the papers.

After only two days on the new drug, Bob's pain escalated. He called the palliative care doctor and was instructed to increase his dosage. That night, he woke up disoriented. I helped him back to bed, worried that he had pushed himself too hard the previous day and might have taken the wrong dosage in confusion. The next morning, I had a hard time waking him up. I began to panic when he couldn't answer the simplest of questions. His speech was slurred and incoherent. *Is he having a stroke?* I called the nurse involved in his home care. She arrived quickly and saw that his lips were blue, indicating his lack of oxygen. "We need to get him to a hospital immediately." She called for an ambulance as I phoned friends to pick up the kids after school and to tell Bob's children to meet us at the hospital. The ride was nerve-racking. *Is this it? The end? No, it's too soon. He was fine yesterday. How could his health decline so quickly? It must be something else, but what if this is it?*

The Emergency Room attendant tried to stop me from entering. "I have information about his medication that the doctors need," I insisted. He let me by him. When I entered the ER, I learned to my horror that the medical team was enacting the DNR protocol. They weren't treating him. Instead, they assumed he wanted the DNR order followed. I couldn't believe what I was seeing. I felt powerless to override the DNR. The attending physician would not reason with me. "I'm sorry, but he signed a DNR," she said. I knew with every fiber in my being that Bob was not ready to die. *For God's sake, we were out for lunch and shopping together yesterday and he was fine! How could he be dying today? Cancer doesn't turn around on a dime like that. This can't be happening.*

I found the oncologist on duty — the one doctor who would listen to me. He agreed that Bob's sudden demise was unusual and asked for a CT scan. The ER's head doctor refused. "Are you the wife?" she asked sternly. "Come with me." She stormed off, without checking whether I was following. I dutifully trailed her to a quieter, more secluded area of the ER, hoping to receive some positive news.

"He's not going to make it through the night," she adamantly stated.

I tried to reason with her, begging her not to give up on him. I tried to appeal to her compassion, telling her about our children. This backfired on me. "You can't bring them here!" she barked. "This is the ER. If they see him like this, they will be psychologically scarred for life."

Bob's life was in her hands. My helplessness switched to anger. *You bitch! Who gives you the right to play God with my husband? And now you want to tell me how to deal with my children? How dare you! They are my children and my husband. I will decide what's best for them.* My mind raced for someone and something that could help. I tried to reach Bob's doctors one by one: first his oncologist, then radiologist, and finally surgeon. None of them was on duty. I tried the palliative care team, but every member of the team was geared towards helping him to end his life. I never felt more powerless and terrified.

I'm Losing You. The Stevie Wright song looped in my head. Everything felt so unreal. *Why is this happening?* With each passing moment, I felt that the man I loved so much was slipping away from me.

Looking back, I can't believe I kept it together as I informed our families and closest friends about Bob's condition, and consulted with his kids. I suggested to his children to phone their mother to come to the hospital to give them support, even though Bob's former wife was not someone I wanted around at that time.

I wasn't sure what to do with our boys. If I sent for them and he did survive, it would cause them undue stress. *If Bob doesn't make it, how will they feel not having had a chance to say goodbye?* The palliative care folks suggested that I might want to ask the boys what they would like to do. That sounded like a reasonable idea, but how do you tell your sons that their father may not make it through the night? While Bob and I had talked with them about Bob's health being poor and the fact that he may not get better and could even die one day, that day always seemed far away.

I phoned my next-door neighbor Graham, who was looking after the boys. I was shaking when Kaiden took the phone. "Honey, Daddy is not doing very well. Would you like to come and see him?" I tried not to scare him too much.

"No, thank you," he replied politely.

Oh no! He doesn't understand the gravity of the situation and he may regret this decision for the rest of his life. I have to be honest with him.

"Honey, Daddy may not make it through the night."

"Okay, I'll come," he replied, sounding shaken.

I had a similar conversation with his brother. About an hour later, Graham arrived with them in their pajamas, clinging to their favorite stuffed animals for courage. The site of the two of them being so vulnerable caused another crack in my heart.

I hugged them both and tried to prepare them. "Are you ready to see him now?"

"Yes," they both said at once, hugging their stuffies tighter.

The ER is not a place anyone wants to die, and certainly not a place for two young boys to say goodbye to their father. The boys had experienced so many hospital rooms and doctors' offices in their young lives, but this was different. It was dark and packed with people, some incoherent.

Bob was awake after being unconscious most of the day. "Hi, pumpkins," he said with a smile as he saw the boys approaching.

"Hi, Daddy," they chimed.

Unaware of the seriousness of his condition, he was surprised to see them. "Isn't it late for you to be here?" He looked at me questioningly.

They both hugged him, in spite of all the wires attached to him. "I love you, Daddy," they each told him.

"Now can we go?" my eldest asked me. "I'm not feeling very well."

I understood. I was barely keeping my last meal down. "Sure. Just say goodbye and then Graham will take you back home."

"Bye, Daddy," they said in unison.

"Bye, boys," Bob replied with a tender smile.

This can't be it. This can't be the last time the boys remember being with their father. I felt more determined than ever to get someone on our side to turn things around. *I will do whatever it takes to make sure the boys see their father again, at home. If he is going to die, it has to be in a better place than this.*

As Bob became more alert, he kept saying that something was wrong. I didn't tell him that the medical team had decided to stop treating him. Fortunately, part way through the night, a new ER doctor came on shift. Her compassion was a soothing balm compared to the evening we had experienced with the ER doctor from hell. The new doctor immediately ordered a CT scan, which later revealed that a large amount of fluid had built up on Bob's remaining lung. That combined with the increased medication had started to shut down his body. His lung was drained the next morning and he was taken off the medication. He began to recover quickly.

I called the boys.

"Did Daddy make it through the night?" they asked in stoic anticipation. I cringed, thinking of the weight that these two young souls had to endure. It didn't seem fair.

"Yes, Daddy is much better," I was delighted to report. "He should be home in a few days." I heard their huge sighs of relief.

The hospital released Bob a couple of days later, refusing to take any responsibility for the way his condition had initially been handled. We felt so relieved but exhausted from the experience. We reviewed every detail to understand what went wrong and how to avoid such a drama from happening again. The ordeal taught us that the DNR approval robbed us of our already limited power and that a hospital was not a good place to die.

CHAPTER 9

Waiting for a Miracle

Bob is gone. I sat on a rock along my favorite path in the woods. An assortment of trees towered over me — maple, birch, ash, pine and oak — all banning together like the League of Nations to protect me. Golden rays of sunlight burst through the trees, offering me healing energy. A chorus of birds soothed my jagged nerves. I felt like an untethered balloon but nature's cathedral kept me grounded and safe. *Where are you, Bob?* I couldn't believe he was dead. *How will I be able to exist on this planet without you?* As I sat there, the last days of Bob's life replayed in my mind.

"There is nothing more we can do. I am sorry." The oncologist tried to deliver the news as gently as possible.

"So this is where we're at?" Bob asked as if receiving the progress report on a project rather than his life. His stoicism surprised me, tugged at my heart.

I reached out for Bob's hand. "How much more time?" I asked the doctor as I held my breath for the answer.

"Two to six months, but probably the former," she replied with tears in her eyes.

We left the hospital for the last time, now on our own and frightened. We no longer had the medical community behind us. We tried to get our heads around the shift from fighting Bob's disease to surrendering to it. We refused at first. For twenty-four hours we racked our brains trying to come up with some other option. The local doctor who was working with Bob's home-care nurses offered him a final 'Hail Mary.' It was a daily injection to try to bolster his immune system. Bob put all of his faith in this last-ditch attempt to save him, but it didn't help. His health declined rapidly. Our plans had to be changed by the moment. We called on family and friends for support. Within hours, troops arrived, our two fridges were filled with meals, and we had multiple offers to help with the kids.

It was difficult to decide whether or not to receive palliative care at home. Bob didn't want the boys to be scarred emotionally by watching him die. The closest palliative care facility was a half-hour drive away, which would have required me being away from the boys a lot more of the time. In the end, the decision was made for us because the palliative care facility was full. Bob's kids, brothers and sisters-in-law all gathered at our house. Thanksgiving was Bob's favorite holiday. Even though it was a week early and he lacked the strength to eat, we cooked a big turkey dinner, knowing he would enjoy the aromas and the family spirit that would surround him throughout the day.

At night, while Bob was sleeping, his brother Leigh sat on the couch next to me with a glass of wine. "I can see he wants to spend every last moment with you. These last few days with the both of you have shown me something I didn't realize — that you have a unique relationship. The way he looks at you, the way you are together... I never really saw it before. Now I see the deep love and respect that exist between you." *Finally, he sees it!* Bob and I had been trying to explain the depth of our connection to his family for years. I felt Bob wanted his brothers to realize it before he died. So I was so relieved that Leigh did.

I decided the boys needed a break and sent each of them to their respective best friend's house for a sleepover. We didn't know whether Bob would make it through the night. So I reminded them to say goodbye to their dad. By this point, Bob was terribly weak and hooked up to an oxygen mask. I watched trying to hold back tears as Bob hugged each son and patted his back lightly.

"Bye, Daddy. I love you," they each said, lacing one small arm around his neck as they each held their stuffed animal in the other — Kaiden with his bat and Kerrsen with his cheetah.

"Goodnight, pumpkins. I love you, too," he replied as he'd done every night of their lives.

Bob and I went to bed that night in the makeshift hospital room we had created for him in the living room. He woke up before dawn, agitated and unable to speak. I tried to make him comfortable as I struggled to understand what he needed. I helped him into his wheelchair and took him into the middle of the family room as he had gestured for me to do. He stared blankly, not appearing to see the autumn beauty outside the row of windows. His face seemed lifeless. I figured he was numbed by the heavy medication he'd been given. Then I wondered for a second whether he was aware of everything around him but simply couldn't communicate. I asked him what he was looking at. "Colors," he managed to say.

Was he seeing the colors of the leaves outside or was it possible that he was seeing my aura? "What colors do you see around me?"

"Orange," he seemed pleased to announce. "More colors!" he added, a bit excited.

I couldn't understand what he was trying to say to me, but I felt it was important to him. I looked down at his wedding ring. It was cutting off the circulation on his swollen finger. I took it off his hand. To assess his clarity, I asked him if he remembered what was engraved on the inside.

"Love will keep us alive," he said slowly.

"Yes, that's right!" I was surprised that he was able to answer me so clearly.

"More love," he said.

Oh God. Does he mean that I didn't show him enough love, that I could have done more? His words haunted me.

The rest of the morning he sat in his favorite reclining chair, eyes closed, his foot gently tapping to the music playing in the background. In the afternoon, we moved him back to the makeshift hospital room so he could lie down. He was given medication to ease his pain and anxiety, and it put him into a peaceful coma. I leaned over and whispered in his ear, "It's okay, my love. You can go now. I will be okay. I'll take good care of our boys. Don't you worry!"

I left the room to let other family members spend a short time with Bob. In the kitchen, I found one of my friends crying as she looked at the fridge magnet that Kerrsen had made for Bob in the shape of a heart with the message: "I wish you could stay longer, Daddy." I turned away, unable to bear the sadness.

I suddenly remembered the Boy Scouts event that Kaiden and Kerrsen were supposed to attend that day. If I had been in a clear state of mind, I would have just ignored the fact they couldn't attend. Instead, I stepped out of the room to phone the organizer. In a fog of grief, I blurted out, "The boys can't make it today because their father is dying." The poor man was silent, not knowing what to say. I was numb at the time to how shocking my words must have been to him. Everything had become surreal as I returned to the kitchen to wait with my friends for Bob to die.

Our friend, Christian, was a doctor who had agreed to be with us during Bob's final moments. It was reassuring to have Christian present in case Bob needed medical support beyond what the home care nurses could provide. He went with me after a few moments to check on Bob.

Leigh glanced up at me. "I think he's gone."

I turned to Christian for confirmation. He checked Bob's neck for a pulse and nodded. "He's gone."

So many emotions rose to the surface — relief that Bob's suffering was finally over, devastation that the love of my life was gone, dread about the impact that his death would have on our boys and my own life. "Can I have a moment alone with him?" I asked.

Everyone quickly cleared the room and made sure the door was closed. I wrapped my arms around Bob's lifeless body, tears streaming down my face. I held him, not wanting to let go. I noticed the song playing softly: *Waiting for a Miracle,* by Bruce Cockburn. I laughed angrily at the irony. *It's too late for a miracle.*

I had anticipated this moment for so long, gone over it in my head a thousand times. I expected to feel his presence. *Where are you, Bob?* I looked around the room. Before he died, I had asked him to give me a sign. *Where is my sign?* I felt nothing. I became impatient. *Maybe I won't feel him after all?* Realizing that quite some time had passed and the others might soon return to check on me, I decided to sneak outside for a few moments to try to recompose myself. It had been raining on and off during the overcast day, but the moment I stepped onto the front porch, the sky brightened with a beam of light dramatically parting the clouds. *There's my sign!*

As I stood in the magic of the moment, torn between immense sadness and awe, my neighbor, Chantal, drove up the street. Her car slowed down as she approached my house. We exchanged glances. I could see from her expression that she understood what had just happened. She hesitated, unsure whether to stop to give me some comfort or to keep going to afford me some time alone. *Please don't stop. I can't speak with anyone right now.* She continued slowly down the road. An hour later she dropped off a poem about that brief moment we had just shared.

Your Doorstep

I drive by your doorstep
nearly every single day.
I wonder how you are doing,
can I help you in any way?
I know your world is changing,
in a grave and sudden way.
I wonder how you are doing,
can I help you in any way?
I saw you on your doorstep
as I drove by again today.
I wondered should I stop
or simply continue on my way.
I left you on your doorstep
on this very sad day.
You seemed to need a moment
in a grave and sudden way.
I'll keep driving by your doorstep
each and every day.
Please let me know if I can help
in any simple way.

I couldn't believe that during the most painful moments of my life I experienced what felt like two miracles: nature seemingly communicating with me through a break in the clouds, and the deep understanding and compassion of another human being. Bruce Cockburn had been right: there was a miracle... Just not the one I hoped.

"Your son is home!" I heard someone behind me say. I looked up to see our friends driving Kaiden toward our house. I had called them a half hour earlier, saying that he needed to return home as soon as possible, but they did not live close by. They had tried to rush but could see by my face that it was too late. The mother of Kaiden's friend gave a look of sincere apology. "It's okay," I managed to say.

I prepared myself as I watched my young son walk up the driveway, oblivious to the sad news I was about to share with him and the dramatic turn his life was about to take. *How can I tell him? What words should I use to soften the blow?* I had rehearsed this a hundred times in my head, but felt powerless in the moment to protect my son from the painful news he was about to receive.

"Honey, sit down beside me," I said.

"What's wrong, Mommy?"

I put my arm around him. "Your Daddy's gone."

Silence as my son tried to digest my words.

"He died a few minutes ago," I said.

"He's gone?"

"Yes, honey. I am so sorry." I started to cry.

"Are you okay, Mommy?"

"Yes, but I am very, very sad. I loved your Daddy so much."

"Kerrsen is home," I heard another voice call up to me. I asked someone to stay with Kaiden while I went to talk to my youngest son. I didn't know how I could go through this a second time. I felt like I was enduring repeated bolts of pain — first with Bob's death, then having to break the news to each of my sons. I didn't think I could handle any more.

Kerrsen bounded up the driveway after being dropped off by friends. He was excited to tell me that he'd had the best day ever because he had acquired a new Pokemon card with "maximum damage." I looked into the beautiful cherub face of my seven-year-old son. *I'm about to turn this into the worst day of his life. I'm about to deliver 'maximum damage.'*

For the second time that day, I sat one of my sons down on the front steps to deliver the shattering news. "Your Daddy died a little while ago."

"Really?" His happy energy turned quiet as he absorbed this information. "When?"

"Just a few minutes ago. I called your friend's parents to ask them to bring you home right away, but Daddy died before you got here. I'm glad you at least had a chance to say goodbye last night."

He nodded in agreement.

I took the boys inside and spent time with them, helping them to process everything. Within a short period of time they'd had enough and asked to be able to go and play. I wished for a similar escape for myself. *I know... I need to go for a walk in the woods with Gunner.* I asked Bob's brothers to make arrangements with the funeral home and made certain that the boys were looked after and out of the house when the undertakers arrived. Then I went back into the room where Bob's body lay to say goodbye for one last time. I held his hand for a moment. I noticed the necklace that he always wore. I removed it and put it around my neck after placing his wedding ring on it. I took a final look at his body.

Every inch of it was already engraved in my memory. I thought of how much I loved his body and how it had brought me such comfort, pleasure and joy. *But this is not the real Bob. This is only a shell. He was still alive somewhere.* This belief made it a bit easier to let go.

"Goodbye, my love. We had an amazing time, didn't we? I will always love you. Our love will keep us alive." I kissed him on the cheek and walked to the door. I turned and blew him a final kiss. I walked out of the house and down the street. I could hear people calling after me to wait for them to join me. I ignored them and rushed onwards. I needed to be alone.

I spent at least an hour sitting in silence on the rock in the woods, rehashing the events of the past few weeks, trying to calm myself, and wondering where Bob was. Unable to console myself, I continued down the path deeper into the woods. A gentle breeze stroked my skin, reminding me I was still alive. The beauty of the autumn forest enveloped me like a familiar blanket. I came upon a favorite spot next to a large pond. The calm water reflected the kaleidoscope of tree colors. I sat on a bench admiring God's handiwork. I realized how perfect it was that I would end up at this spot. Bob had been pivotal in saving the pond a few years earlier when one of its banks had partially eroded, emptying a lot of the water into an adjoining stream. As a town councilor, he'd worked hard to broker a deal between the municipality and local homeowners to invest in a dam that would prevent a total erosion and the pond's eventual disappearance. I felt so connected to Bob as I sat next to the dam he'd succeeded in having built. *So this is what's left when we die: our life's work.*

I took out my phone and snapped a shot. I immediately thought it was strange that I would take a photo on the worst day of my life. Then again, as I looked at this picture-perfect scene and felt so close to Bob, I was reminded that even in my darkest hour I was surrounded by extraordinary beauty. *I am going to be all right. I can still experience joy in a world without Bob.* I knew I would need a reminder of this in the future. I hoped the photo would do just that.

Part 3

"*When a loved one dies, it activates within us a strong desire to be in the Vortex in a stronger way than anything else that can happen.*"

– Abraham Hicks

CHAPTER 10
Somewhere in Time

I feel so listless. I don't care how I look, what I eat, who comes to see me. The conversations around me hold no interest. I am numb as I greet the waves of people arriving at my home to pay their respects. One after the other gives me a hug, asks how I am doing. *How do you think I'm doing? I am trapped in my worst nightmare and I can't wake up,* I want to scream but don't. I see so much love and compassion pouring out of all these people, so I smile and thank them for their kindness. Everything is slow motion. I struggle to keep up, but the voices are distorted, like they are under water. I stand feeling the hole in my chest that no one else sees and endure my exposed heart beating all of my joy, confidence and hope away.

The simplest task can set off an explosion of emotions. As I rummage through the mudroom closet, one of Bob's tan loafers falls out. Seeing the well-worn leather of his favorite shoes pierces my heart. I can almost see the foot that is supposed to be in it, and the toned leg and the rest of the body that should still be with me. Yet, here the shoe is, sitting deserted on the floor. The loafer reminds me of a summer night walking hand in hand down our street. I also remember the shoes being kicked off on a sandy beach during our last Florida trip. I remember watching our toddler shuffling around our apartment with his father's enormous shoes. Bob will never walk in those shoes again. I will never live the life I had imagined with him. His clothes, guitar, tools, bike, car and so much more remain as a reminder of my crushed dreams and the burden of carrying on without him.

I keep busy with funeral arrangements and looking after my children and guests. I promise myself I won't cry at Bob's funeral. Not that I don't want to show emotion, but I feel it should be a time of honoring Bob, celebrating his life. I want to give the eulogy. I know him best.

As I look at the somber faces of my family and friends in the packed church, I marvel at the impact his life had on so many individuals. I want them to smile, just like I am, even though my heart is breaking. Bob would have wanted us to be happy.

When I first try to speak, I start to shake. Tears run down my face. My sons are next to me at the altar. Kerrsen hugs me. "Don't cry, Mommy," he says loud enough for everyone to hear. I note the church fills with sighs. I smile, hug him tightly, take a deep breath and begin again. To my surprise, I manage to convey most of what I want to say. "Thank you, Bobby, for the most amazing fifteen-year love affair," I conclude. "I will miss you terribly."

Bob's next oldest brother, Chris, sings *Imagine*. He and Bob had sung together for more than 40 years. Chris's first performance without Bob moves many of us to tears. Father Demers had asked Kim and Stacy, Bob's daughters, to read Bible passages, but they wanted to share more personal messages. Father Demers is visibly flustered when they go off script and read their own tributes to their father.

Kevin, Bob's adult son, and our young boys each light a candle to symbolize their intention to have their father's love and work continue within them.

I had encouraged my friends to bring their children. Many were hesitant because their youngsters had never been to a funeral. It is my sons' first funeral, too. I want them to be comforted by their young friends. Halfway through the ceremony, dozens of children like nymphs pour out of the pews carrying stuffed animals under their arms. They walk up to the altar and lay each one into a basket as a gift of love and comfort for my boys. My friend, Judy, organized these "baskets of hugs" so my sons could each dive into their own basket whenever they were aching for their father and wanted to feel the community's love and support. The children flowing down the aisle and surrounding my boys will be remembered forever by everyone at the church. When Judy whispers to Kaiden about having a lot of friends, he smiles. "I didn't even need to invite them! They just came for me!"

From the choir loft, a dear friend with a deep tenor voice sings *Across the Universe*. The words lift me, give me hope. *I am going to be okay. My world is going to be okay.*

As we carry Bob's ashes out of the church, there are hundreds of other people waiting for us outside along with a local fire truck with its lights flashing. Flags have been lowered to half-mast to honor Bob and his contribution to our town as one of its councilors.

After the celebration of life at the local community center and a few smaller family gatherings over the next few days, people began returning home to their normal lives, but I could not. My normal life was gone forever. The solitude arrived with many dreaded firsts: morning coffee for one, dinner for three, Sunday brunch at our local diner followed by a visit to the park without Dad. Thanksgiving, a holiday we always cherished as family time, arrived only a day after saying our final goodbyes to Bob. I couldn't believe I had to face my first holiday without him so soon.

My mother delayed her flight home out of concern for me. Although we both felt such grief, we decided to celebrate the holiday, for my boys' sake. We revisited the local farm where Bob had gone with the boys and me in past years to pick apples and pumpkins and enjoy hayrides as a family. My body was like an anvil. It took all my strength just to move one foot in front of the other. I wanted to curl up somewhere and escape into sleep, but I kept going for my kids. Kaiden later dragged me to the grocery store, determined to find all the food for a perfect Thanksgiving dinner. He was so sweet, but I couldn't bear the idea of making a special dinner a week after Bob's passing. I forced myself to follow Kaiden around the store as if treading chest-high mud. Kaiden filled the cart as I picked out a ready-to-serve chicken, boxed mashed potatoes and stuffing, and cans of gravy and cranberry sauce. I knew this would be all I could muster in terms of preparing dinner. Kaiden didn't seem to notice that this wasn't our traditional homemade dinner. He was happy to be given the responsibility of helping me to organize and shop for the meal. Mom and the boys tried to make the dinner festive, setting out autumn leaves and candles on the table. I felt a mixture of pride in my sons who were demonstrating incredible maturity, and shame at myself for struggling to complete the smallest tasks.

My next dreaded first was our eleventh wedding anniversary. Instead of celebrating it together as we had done for the past decade, I went to get his ashes at the funeral parlor. The mere thought of picking them up any earlier was too upsetting, but I didn't want to mark our anniversary without some part of him present. Back home in the room where he died, I held the linen box of ashes with his picture on it in my arms and sobbed. How could this be all that was left of the man who was my whole life? *He really is gone,* I realized yet again. I felt so alone. The weight of the loneliness against my chest made it difficult to breathe. I thought back to that beautiful day in Bali when we exchanged vows by the Indian Ocean. I remembered feeling slight trepidation in the midst of all the beauty and joy of that day. I feared I might lose him one day, along with all of my happiness. *Was I just afraid that something this special couldn't last? Did I feel guilt for all the pain that had been caused so that we could be together? Or had I somehow foreseen this sad anniversary eleven years in the future?* I wasn't sure.

I decided to organize a special dinner in Bob's honor. The boys helped me to pick out the meal. Bob always made Sloppy Joes for them on their birthdays, so they assumed he would want the same for this dinner. I was pleased they wanted to continue his favorite traditions. It made me feel he was still a part of our family. I wanted to make his popular recipe, but he never wrote it down. I called his brother Chris to see if he knew it from their earlier years together. No luck. *Another thing lost forever.* The loss added to my grief.

Prior to Bob's death, we tried to obtain a legal marriage certificate. It was never important to Bob or me before he became ill. We assumed our Bali marriage would be considered legal in Canada and never bothered to obtain a Canadian document to confirm it. As Bob's condition worsened, we wanted to be certain that we were married under Canadian law, just in case. The process was more complicated than we had expected. It required multiple visits to a notary's office, translating our Balinese marriage certificate into English, and Bob and I each filling out forms and signing affidavits. The months the whole process took resulted in the Canadian certificate only being delivered after Bob died. The notary called me into her office. As I sat down, she looked sadly at me, acknowledging the empty seat that Bob had filled during previous visits. She hesitated to open the file in front of her. "I must warn you," she said as she pulled out the marriage certificate. I glanced across the table and gasped when I saw what had been stamped in large bold letters across the document: Marriage dissolved due to death.

"My marriage is dissolved?" I asked in shock. *How could that be?* I didn't feel unmarried. I still wore my wedding ring. I continued to feel a profound physical connection in my heart to Bob. I never referred to myself as a widow or single. *I was Bob's wife. I always would be.* I wondered how a person could go from being totally in love and feeling such a full emotional connection and commitment to a spouse one day and be deemed unmarried the next.

"He is still my husband, not my ex-husband," I protested. "I don't know how to turn that off." The notary looked at me with sympathetic eyes but had no reassuring words.

The words "until death do us part" came to mind. *Isn't that what we had promised each other?* my rational mind asked. *Yes, but death didn't end my feelings of love and commitment,* my heart replied. Bureaucracy regarded our marriage as having a precise beginning and a definite end. By contrast, I felt that my love for Bob and my relationship with him were infinite. Legally, everything that had been ours was now mine. Our children, our home, even our cars belonged to me alone. Despite the logic of this, I didn't like it one bit. I loved sharing my life and everything in it with Bob. I felt burdened with the responsibility of now carrying everything on my own.

I spiraled downwards. I didn't know how to stop myself. I was being pulled into grief's darkness. I tried to resist, to push it away, to ignore it, but succumbed to the sweet relief of its self-pitying powerlessness. I'd been fighting for so long to stay in control, strong and positive, that I couldn't do it anymore. I believed that Bob still existed in some way, but I didn't know how to connect with him. I picked up the phone and dialed his cell, just to hear his voicemail message. I willed him to answer. *Come to me, Bobby. Show yourself,* I pleaded. *You promised you would!*

Nothing. I couldn't see him, couldn't hear him, couldn't feel his presence.

Another first without Bob was a weekend trip to visit my sister and her family in Toronto. The plan for Saturday was for us to visit the Body World Exhibition at the Ontario Science Centre. I did not vote for seeing preserved human bodies that had been dissected to display the cardiovascular and circulatory systems. It seemed insensitive to me that this would even be suggested as an activity. I worried about how my boys would feel about going to such an exhibit only a few weeks after seeing their father's lifeless body. However, majority ruled and we went. The exhibition was called *The Story of the Heart*. As we plodded through the hordes of visitors, I felt the now familiar weight in my chest. I looked at the bodies and wondered what their lives had been like, and who had loved these people and still missed them. It felt so disrespectful to be gawking at their dissected bodies. Yet similar to a horror movie that both frightens and captivates us, the exhibits roused a morbid curiosity in me and ended up teaching me a lot. One exhibit in particular caught my attention: a woman, looking forlorn into the distance, head partially lowered, shoulders rounded. She looked sad even without the skin to mold her features or the magic of life to animate her eyes. "Died of a broken heart," the plaque beside her read. "The human heart is a mysterious muscle, a hard-working organ and the most complex system in the body. The heart is connected to the rest of the body even on an emotional and philosophical level." *A broken heart is a real phenomenon?* I had wondered if this was possible. I felt like I was looking in a mirror. Kaiden was holding my hand this whole time. I had almost forgotten he was next to me when he said, "That looks like you, Mom."

Oh, my God, he has noticed how terrible I feel. My nine-year-old son has seen through my brave front. I guess I am not fooling anyone.

The exhibition and Kaiden's observation confirmed what I had already suspected: my longing for Bob consumed my every thought. I wanted to follow my husband to wherever it is that we go after death. I knew if I continued on this course, eventually my body would succumb to my broken heart. Disease would devour me. Or I would be in a serious accident.

An image pops into my head: Bob and I are looking through a two-way mirror, watching the boys. They can't see us. They look sad and scared, alone without both of their parents. I'm unable to touch them, to comfort them. I realize this is what it would be like if I died. The thought of not being able to connect with my children, to care for and guide them is more than I can bear. No matter how much I miss Bob, my life is now with our boys. They need me, and I need them. I realize I have an important mission to continue with them as their mother and sole parent. This vision inspired me to begin to do whatever it took to heal myself and to make a new life for the three of us.

Even though I had made up my mind to remain present and healthy for the boys, I still wanted so much to find a way to communicate with Bob, but I had no idea how to do so. Each day, I looked for signs, wondering if any were coming from him, or my imagination. After a particularly trying day, I sat quietly in the room where Bob had taken his last breath and said aloud, "How am I going to do this without you, Bobby? How can I raise our kids, look after the household and get my life back in order without you? You were my rock, my sidekick, my go-to person for everything. Hell, you were my life partner, my business partner, and my parenting partner! I leaned on you when times were difficult, and you always knew just the right thing to say."

"You need to rally," his voice said in my head.

What? Was that my imagination? Is it possible that Bob is trying to communicate with me? I expected to hear his voice with my ears or to see him with my eyes. Instead I heard his voice way inside my brain. Almost imperceptible, but I knew it wasn't coming from my conscious self. The idea of rallying was the furthest idea from my mind at that point.

Bob used to say "We need to rally!" each time his disease presented a new challenge. It was his way of shining a positive light on the situation, of infusing hope. When the doctors stated there was nothing more they could do, I heard Bob say one last time, "We have to find a way to rally." My heart broke knowing he meant that we needed to prepare the family and then focus on Bob having a 'good death' experience, surrounded by his loved ones in a peaceful and comfortable setting.

Was I really hearing from him now, or just imagining his voice by recalling his words? I wasn't sure.

"Bob, I have always had you around to help me rally. How can I rally alone?" I said aloud.

"You don't have to," came the reply immediately in that same voice of his from somewhere deep inside my head. "I am here with you."

I didn't expect that response. *Is it possible? Is this a way to communicate with him? Maybe our new language is an internal nudging that I can tune into like a radio frequency. Maybe it won't be through my five senses, as I had imagined, but rather through subtler senses, if they actually exist.* The heaviness within my chest lifted a bit. Later that day, I heard a song from the *Somewhere in Time* movie soundtrack. One of the many coincidences Bob and I noticed early in our relationship was our mutual love of this obscure movie. Starring Christopher Reeve and Jane Seymour, it was the love story of two people trapped in different time frames. Elise lived in the early nineteen-hundreds and Richard in the nineteen-seventies. At the beginning of the movie, a very old Elise finds young Richard just before she dies, and pleads with him to 'come back' to her. Not understanding what this meant, he is compelled to discover the answers. He eventually uses his scientific skills to travel back in time to find her. I now wondered if Bob and I were stuck in different dimensions. *Could I find a bridge back to him, too? Was this the reason we both loved this movie so much? Had it been planted somehow in our subconscious minds like a key to a hidden treasure chest?*

CHAPTER 11

Ill Stand by You

One day, while on a nearby hiking trail, I noticed that our town had finally completed a boardwalk across a protected wetlands area. Bob had been working on this project for three years. *Bob would be so proud,* I thought. *I wish he could have seen it completed.*

"I do see it, and it looks great!" I heard Bob respond in my head. His voice was coming through more frequently now. It had a different quality than my own thoughts. It was softer, kinder, more loving. Ideas would pop into my head that weren't quite like me, but were definitely the kind of things that Bob would say.

A couple of days later, I was preparing to go out for dinner with four of our closest friends. We had always socialized together as couples. On this particular evening, I would be the fifth wheel. Both couples had very close relationships with their partners, making Bob's absence all the more pronounced. *Bobby, I wish you were joining us tonight.* Immediately, I heard, "I will be there with you all." Alone in the bathroom, I looked around in search of that voice. "And, might I add, you look wonderful tonight." The line from Eric Clapton's song brought me to tears. It was a song that Bob sang often to me. It reminded me of a party we attended a year earlier. As we entered the crowded restaurant, he slid his hand in mine and said, "You look beautiful!" I felt a mixture of comfort, security and pride with him at my side. The crowd swallowed us up and we quickly became separated. I glanced across the room. He instinctively looked up and smiled back at me. Before long, he was back at my side. "Can I get you something, babe?" he asked softly, as he kissed my neck. When we returned home that evening, we chatted about the night's events. "You were the most beautiful woman in the room," he insisted. "I couldn't keep my eyes off you." Even after a decade of marriage and two kids, he looked at me with such love.

Oh God, how am I ever going to live without him? I cried as I stared into the bathroom mirror, fresh mascara smudging my face.

Each morning, I woke up to my new reality. Sadness and dread jolted me out of a peaceful slumber. It was the opposite of a nightmare. All I wanted to do was return to sleep, to my illusionary world where everything was still okay. I couldn't bear to lift myself out of bed, let alone look after the boys. Our morning routine was so difficult without my partner. We used to run the morning like a well-oiled machine together. Now making breakfast, preparing lunches and getting the boys dressed and out the door on my own drained all of my energy.

I began noticing that the clock radio always woke me up to

a song that helped to ease my pain. One morning it was James Taylor reassuring me that I had a friend. The next day to Bowie's promise that he would stick with me into my golden years. The following morning Sting delivered a message in a bottle, helping me to see that I was not alone in my pain and that love could mend my broken heart. It made me suspect that Bob had found a way to soothe me during these difficult moments at dawn.

There was one song I heard repeatedly throughout the first few weeks after Bob died. It was Chrissie Hynde's, *I'll Stand by You*. It had been a hit when Bob and I met fifteen years earlier. If I didn't know better, I would have thought it was a current hit, because I heard it play multiple times during the day on the radio at home, in the car, at the grocery store and on my computer and mobile devices. It reminded me that Bob would never desert me.

One evening the sound of my iPhone playing downstairs in the kitchen woke me up. I jumped out of bed and shuffled down the stairs, half asleep. *Was I dreaming?* Mysteriously, my iPhone was playing *I'll Stand by You. How had it switched on by itself and how had it landed on this song from a thousand on my playlist? Was this pure coincidence? Or Bob trying to connect with me again?* I was reminded of the movie *Ghost* with Patrick Swayze playing a spirit who tries to make his presence known to his girlfriend through various means. Bob knew I loved this movie and felt particularly connected to Swayze and his real-life wife who together struggled with Patrick's cancer. He died just three weeks before Bob. I wondered if Bob was playing ghost to let me know he was still watching over me.

Another night, I heard a man and a woman talking downstairs.

I went down and found my iPhone playing the middle of a podcast. After noting the time on the recording for some reason, I turned the phone off and went back to sleep. The next morning, when I listened to the podcast at that same time juncture, I was amazed to discover that the discussion focused on the increasing research in support of a soul existing beyond the life of a body. *Was this Bob again trying to reach out to me the way I suspected he was with the timing of some radio songs?*

Bob had a deep connection with music. He loved to play the guitar and sing. I marveled at how he could play a song after just a few minutes of listening to it. He hadn't picked up his guitar for a long time before we met. I encouraged him to play, and even bought him an acoustic guitar, which he loved. It made sense to me that his spirit would try to communicate with me through music. As I clued into the possibility of my iPhone being a way for Bob to connect with me, I carried it with me everywhere. In the middle of a song, the iPhone would often make a blip sound and change tunes. Each time, without fail, the new song would have lyrics with a message I needed right then or related to something I was pondering at the time. The idea of Bob still looking out for me lifted my spirits. These occurrences became more frequent as I started tuning into them.

I still wasn't sure whether the messages were anything more than coincidences or my mind playing tricks on me. One of my friends came over most mornings to go for a walk or accompany me to yoga class. One morning, after a walk in the woods, we sat in my kitchen sipping coffee. I told her about the subtle voices I had been hearing and the coincidental music. "I thought I would see Bob appear right in front of me or something substantial like that," I said.

"Maybe the language of Spirit is more subtle," she suggested.

In that instant, we heard a huge crash upstairs. Alone in the house, we initially stared at each other in surprise, then burst into laughter. "That wasn't very subtle, was it?" I said with her prompt agreement. When we investigated, we discovered that my aptly named cat, Spirit, had knocked down a bunch of seashells from a bathroom windowsill. *Had Bob prompted Spirit?*

Other messages appeared in a steady stream of dreams, lights flickering, and other electrical and computer-related malfunctions. Any one situation could logically be explained away, but the large number of occurrences led me to believe that I was living on a precipice between two worlds: one that everyone recognized as 'real' and filled with regret, sorrow and pain for me; and, smidgens of another that most people don't perceive, filled with light, mystery and hope.

Nevertheless, I still felt so alone in my grief. I didn't know where to turn. I read books about death and the afterlife to help me to come to terms with my sorrow. I was looking for a template for grieving, one that would allow me to explore the spiritual aspects of Bob's death.

My friends were all supportive, but their lack of shared experience made me feel isolated in my pain. I tried grief counseling, hoping it would alleviate my suffering. I attended a group for women with young children who had lost their husbands. The women in the group, for the most part, were just beginning to come to terms with the sudden loss of their husbands. I, on the other hand, had started my grieving eighteen months earlier when Bob was first diagnosed as terminal. Seeing these women in the early stages of grief, struggling with denial and anger, actually made me appreciate the opportunity I had to grieve alongside Bob during his illness. I was at a different point in my grieving process and knew that I wouldn't significantly benefit from this group.

Still aching for help with my grief, I tried another group. This one specialized in individuals who'd lost a loved one to cancer. Most had lost an elderly parent, rather than a spouse. Once again I didn't feel like I fit. Still, I tried. All the strange coincidences that I had been witnessing encouraged me to explore spirituality and the afterlife. When I mentioned anything of this nature to the group, I was quickly shut down. After two sessions, I quit going.

I instinctively knew that I couldn't escape from grief's soul-crushing grip, no matter how much I wanted to ease its weight. I felt certain that I had to work through my loss and pain, even if I had to do so on my own. Until Bob's death, I hadn't experienced major loss in my life. Yet somehow I always felt its insidious presence lurking around the corner, waiting for me, for my turn. For a long time I held the illusion that if I were good enough or smart enough, I could avoid pain. As I mourned, I saw a similar fear reflected in the eyes of the people around me. They looked at me with compassion, but behind their empathy, I could almost hear them saying to themselves, *Thank God it's not me going through that.*

I assumed at some point I would ask, "Why me?" But it never

happened. I had read Viktor Frankl's *Man's Search for Meaning*, describing his time as a prisoner in a Nazi concentration camp. He observed that the people who were the most resilient and survived the worst trauma were those who found meaning in their experience. His book reaffirmed my belief that there was a purpose for everything in life, including death. So there had to be a reason for Bob's death. I didn't know what it was, but I was determined to figure it out, so that Bob hadn't die in vain.

Despite my unproductive experience with grief counseling, I was still hopeful that it would help my kids. We attended a bereavement camp for children. Most of the kids had lost a parent to cancer, cardiovascular disease or suicide. On the first night, we joined the large circle of children and adults. One by one, the children introduced themselves and shared their story. I was struck by the depth of their young loss, as each child shared one heart-rending story after another.

At the same time, I was inspired. After Bob's death, a number of people reassured me that my boys would be okay – that children are more resilient than adults. My experience at the camp proved this to me. A ten-year-old boy proudly showed me his drawing of a phoenix rising from the ashes with a clear understanding of how this metaphor related to his life.

Another youngster, whose father had been murdered, ran up and down the camp singing *Hey Soul Sister* all weekend, filling the halls with his joyful voice. A young girl, who had lost her father to suicide, generously shared hugs and tried earnestly to meditate next to me. A teenage boy who had lost his father just as he was becoming a man himself was the leader and mentor to all the younger children. One young boy, who had lost his mother and was afraid of the dark, helped me to find my way down a long path to the beach at night with his flashlight. This helped my boys to understand that they were not alone and that other kids had suffered loss, some worse than their own.

If outsiders had peeked into the camp, they would have seen a bunch of youngsters running, laughing, getting into trouble, just being kids. They wouldn't have noticed anything different about them from other children. It reminded me of the time I had spent in the developing world working for an international aid organization. I met children who lived in extreme poverty, near war zones, in dire circumstances. Yet, what I saw there, and again at the grief camp, was children's incredible resilience.

My children's ability to be present, to live with open hearts, honestly, freely, with joy, helped them to deal with their loss and inspired me to do the same. They each intuitively developed their own coping strategies. "I have decided not to be sad anymore," Kaiden announced to me one day. Instead, he filled his days with play, adventure and fun. This was how he intuitively healed.

At first, the boys were hesitant to mention anything about their father for fear that it might upset me or them. By contrast, I spoke about Bob every day. Within a short period of time, they were able to bring him into our conversations and even make jokes and laugh about him. In the car, while driving one of their friends home, I heard them talking about a large shark. "My father is bigger than that shark," the friend said. Not wanting to miss an opportunity to compete, Kerrsen insisted his Dad was even larger.

Listening to him made me realize how much grief he still had to work through, and my heart ached for him. Kaiden didn't hesitate to correct him. "No, he's not anymore. Daddy is only the size of a box," referring to Bob's remains. They all laughed. I was sad that this was our new normal, but I was relieved and filled with pride at how quickly they appeared to be bouncing back.

While I cooked supper one night, Kerrsen told me that a classmate was sad because her father was in Europe on a business trip and she missed him. "It's worse for me, because I haven't seen my Dad in months, and won't ever again," he added. I froze, wanting to do something to take away the pain. I felt helpless, not knowing what to say, but a moment later he asked me: "What's for dinner?" He knew how to acknowledge his feelings of loss and then continue with his life.

Days of the week, like the seasons, each have a particular feel or flavor for me. Bob died on a Sunday. During the first year after his passing, each Sunday brought me back to that day. One Sunday, the door burst open with the sounds of excited young boys filling the room. "Mom, we have a mouse…. He's almost dead," Kaiden said, adding that our cat Spirit had probably caught the mouse.

When I looked into the faces of my two sons and their friend, I saw their immense compassion and eagerness to help the little injured animal. With some degree of difficulty, I stifled my conditioned response to scream *Get that thing out of my house!* and instead asked: "What do you want to do with him?"

"I don't think he'll survive," said Kerrsen. The other two nodded in agreement.

"We should put him out of his suffering," Kaiden suggested.

"But how are we going to do that?" their friend asked.

"Maybe we should make him comfortable until he dies," Kerrsen offered. The other two sighed with relief.

"I know what to do," Kaiden piped up. "I know a lot about death!"

The boys proceeded to transform a shoebox into a makeshift palliative care facility for the ailing mouse, with soft tissues for bedding, food, a Handle with Care sign and a lid with air holes to ensure the cat didn't go after the mouse again. I was surprised when all three of them sat around the box quietly as if in prayer or meditation. "Let's imagine the mouse in healthier, happier times," said Kaiden, sounding deceptively grown up.

"Let's move him into the Spirit Room," said Kerrsen, referring to the room in which his father had died. I had since converted it into a quiet area for meditation and prayer and named it the Spirit Room. Kerrsen's recognition of the sacredness of the space was incredibly moving to me.

They left the mouse, which they named Ralph, to lie quietly while they went outside to play. A half hour later, they returned to discover that the mouse had died. They reacted calmly.

"We could bury him in the shoebox," suggested Kaiden.

"That would be wasteful," stated their eco-conscious friend.

They discussed the option of burning him and saving his ashes or burning an offering of cheese instead, but remembered they weren't allowed to play with matches. So they settled on burying the little critter directly in the ground and placing a rock as a headstone.

When they returned from the woods after burying Ralph, they had lemonade and leftover cake while they discussed their experiences with the mouse. It was amazing how they had re-enacted the whole death ritual from comforting the dying to burial and then a celebration of life all on their own.

The fact that the boys were modeling what they had experienced with death in such a positive way touched me deeply.

As they rode off on their bikes, putting the incident behind them, I looked at the clock: 2:11 p.m. – exactly the time on a Sunday months earlier when I had said my last goodbye to Bob. It occurred to me that the Universe had offered me a beautiful distraction and a subtle reminder of the magic and interconnectedness of all things in nature and our lives.

CHAPTER 12
If God Will Send His Angels

I lie in bed, trying to fall asleep. The dark silence has reminded me of the first night that Bob and I had slept in our new country home. We were amazed at the lack of sound other than the house occasionally creaking on that frigid February night. We had become accustomed to the city's honking cars, screeching emergency sirens, and constant urban hum. I had felt a peaceful release as I snuggled into my husband's arms. Now the silence amplified the empty space as I lay alone in our king-size bed.

I switched on a lamp. Next to a stack of self-help and spiritual books sat the *Healing with the Angels* Oracle Cards created by Doreen Virtue. My yoga instructor had given them to me after Bob died. I hadn't previously noticed that the deck consisted of forty-four cards. The number four held great significance for Bob and me. We were both the fourth child in our birth families.

We started our relationship in 1994. We were married – almost to the day – four years later. We each were born in the fourth month of the year, as was our first baby together, Kaiden, who is Bob's fourth child. In our first corporate training workshop together, we did an emotional intelligence evaluation, and we both fell into the fourth quadrant, which meant we were each results-driven. We often teased each other about being too "four-like." He was forty-four when we met. I was 31 (3+1=4). We were 13 (1+3=4) years apart in age. According to numerology, my life path number is 4 and his was 8 (2x4). And, he died on a fourth of October.

After shuffling the deck, I dealt the following four cards onto the bed: *New Beginnings, Celebration, Divine Guidance and Archangel Michael.* The cards suggested that a clean slate was being presented to me. According to the Tarot, there was cause for celebration as I embarked on new beginnings with fresh opportunities. The angels were surrounding me with loving energy. I was instructed to call upon them whenever I felt afraid. They would help to give me the courage to overcome any fear. The cards were so in keeping with my life circumstances that I couldn't help but think that maybe I was communicating with angels, my late husband or even God.

The next day, I woke up excited but skeptical about the oracle messages. Years of analytic training were hindering my ability to trust what I was experiencing. I wanted confirmation. I asked for more signs to prove this wasn't just my imagination. I took Gunner into the woods to contemplate the messages and walked to where two paths intersect by my favored circle of towering trees. This council of elders deep in the forest is where I had earlier received messages that helped me to prepare for Bob's death. "Okay, you gave me good advice earlier," I said, looking up at these treetops. "What have you to say to me now? Are the messages I'm receiving real or is this all a figment of my imagination?" Just as previously, a single word came immediately to mind. This time, it was: listen. I asked what that meant. Was I not listening properly? Did I have to listen more intently or often? I didn't quite understand, but no other message came to me.

When I arrived home, I decided to consult the oracle cards again. As soon as I picked them up, the *Listening* card fell onto the floor in front of me. When I saw the card I laughed out loud. *Yes, you are communicating with your angels and the messages you are receiving are real,* it read. *By drawing this card, the angels ask you to give up all your doubts. Know that you are truly communicating with heaven, and enjoy the conversation.* I couldn't believe the 'coincidence.' I felt a sense of awe, that I was starting to peek into a magical world that had been hidden from me for a long time, probably since my childhood.

A couple of days later, I came across a stained-glass decoration with the single word *Believe* on it. I bought it and put it in my kitchen window as a constant reminder to do as the angels had instructed.

My friend Debbie picked me up to go out for dinner at a local bistro a few weeks later. At a quiet table, she looked at me compassionately while taking a sip of wine. "I was telling a friend the other day that I have only seen the kind of love that Bob and you shared in one or two other couples," she said. "You were very lucky to have had that."

I sat back in my seat, letting her words comfort me like a warm hug. Debbie is the kind of friend who always makes you feel like you really matter. She listens intently, and only once you're finished talking, speaks softly, offering sage advice, never pushing her point of view. Her mannerisms earn your trust quickly. She had told me over the years that she was gifted with the ability to communicate with people who had died. "You know he's with you now, eh?" She smiled with excitement in her deep brown eyes. Her delicate face, her feathery blond hair, and the graceful way she carried herself gave me the sense I was communicating with an angel.

My heart quickened with excitement. "You think so?"

While Debbie had told me that she was a medium, I had never previously experienced her gift. Now I was relieved that someone else sensed Bob's spirit. I had been telling friends and family members about the coincidences and subtle voices in my head. Most everyone just politely smiled and nodded.

"I saw him in your garden when I came to pick you up," she said. "The sky was bright with the moonlight, so I could see the garden well. I wondered if I were in your shoes whether I would keep my gardens so tidy."

My breath caught in my throat. Kaiden and I had just planted tulip bulbs. As we dug into the earth, I explained to him the purpose: "Like these bulbs, we have entered a dark time in our lives – a time of deep sadness and mourning. These bulbs are to remind us that our spring will come. In a few months, when the snow melts and the flowers begin to poke out of the earth, it will be a sign of a new beginning for us."

Debbie's voice brought me back to the present. "He's concerned about you and the boys, but he's confident that you will be okay." Her gentle tone and kind words soothed me. "He wants you to know that he'll be with you as long as you need him. He no longer experiences time and space the way we do. So, when he is with you, it doesn't preclude him from his own journey in any way."

Her message gave me such relief. I had come to believe that I was sensing Bob's presence and connecting with him, but I was scared it wouldn't last. I had heard a lot of different beliefs about what happens after a person dies. The one that worried me the most was the belief that a soul remains in our realm for only a short time to help family members with the transition, after which the connection is severed. The thought of having a limited amount of time with Bob in this way made me terribly anxious. I couldn't bear the thought of a further separation from him.

Debbie and I spoke all that evening about intuition, spirituality, and the existence of past lives. When I stood to leave, she agreed to do a reading for me. I couldn't contain my excitement over the idea of being able to communicate with Bob again. A second chance to say goodbye.

When Debbie came over to my house for the reading a couple of weeks later, I was excited and nervous. *Will this work? Will he come through?* Debbie had warned me that she was a bit rusty at channeling and wasn't certain she would be able to make a connection. As we settled onto the living room couch, Debbie closed her eyes and drew a long, deep breath to go within.

My heart raced.

"I sense he's here." She laughed, bringing a hand to her mouth as if to politely conceal a burp. "He says he wishes he could have had a bite of the burger that I ate in a hurry earlier so I could get here on time."

I laughed, too. "That certainly sounds like him: his humor and his appetite for burgers. So how does this work? Do I ask you the questions?"

"You can ask him directly." She nodded to an invisible person. "He is giving me some images. These are ways that you can confirm it's him. He is saying 'cousin,' I think? I'm sorry... I'm a little rusty. The images are coming quickly. He understands and will slow down. I am having trouble with the second word. He's saying something about an aunt."

My mother's cousin, Aunt Kathy, used to say *cusa-vinny*, a made-up phrase to get our attention in public. Bob and I adapted this to Cousin Vinny as our parent code to stop the other from saying anything inappropriate when the boys were in earshot. They often asked us who Cousin Vinny was. We would laugh and say he was a cousin they had never met. When I heard Debbie say the word "cousin" in reference to my aunt, I knew we had connected with Bob.

"He's also showing me a Buddha's head on a table with a light. He says he was there with you. Do you know what he is referring to?" she asked.

Astonished, I related to Debbie how the previous night I had placed the box containing his ashes on the desk in the room where he had died. I also made a small shrine with family pictures, candles, a wooden carving of a Buddha's head, and a light. As I switched off this light, I blew a kiss toward his photo and said, "Good night, love." That very instant I experienced a vivid flashback of Bob slowly walking down a hospital corridor away from me. His light blue sweatshirt and jeans hung loosely on his thinned frame. "The image was so real, as if he was right in front of me," I told Debbie. "I longed to go back to that time, because even though it was so difficult, he was still with me. I wondered last night if this was his way – with mental images – of indicating he was with me."

"Yes, he is confirming this," she replied.

My head swirled. *He's really here with me. I wonder how he's doing. I wonder what he thinks of the way I am managing with the boys...*

"Vundabar," she blurted out.

"Why did you just say that?"

"I don't know. He just said that to me."

"It appears that he can read my thoughts!" I said after explaining that he'd answered my internal question.

Bob shared other messages through Debbie about our relationship, the boys, his kids and his mother. He described how our relationship – and even his death – had been mapped out before we were born.

"Can you ask him how I can receive messages directly from him more clearly?"

Debbie concentrated, eyes shut. "He is showing me a candle. He says, 'Light a candle. Use it to center yourself and quiet your mind. Meditate. To connect with me, write down your thoughts and questions. I will answer you.'"

"He is showing me a book," Debbie continued. "Your book. A book about your story together. He says he will write it with you."

"I will do that," I said eagerly. "Tell him I love him and miss him."

"He says, 'I love you, too, and like an eternal flame, our love cannot be extinguished by the death of the body.'

"He says that he is always with you."

I started to cry. "Oh, I miss you so much, Bob."

I walked Debbie out, feeling better than I had since Bob had died. I read and reread the notes I had scribbled as Debbie spoke.

In the days following the reading, I shared the experience with some close friends. When Debbie next called me, she was upset. One of my friends had told her husband, and he reprimanded Debbie at church that Sunday, telling her that she wasn't helping me, that I needed to "move on." I was furious at his meddling. I worried the couple had ruined my chances of communicating with Bob through Debbie again. I also hated the term 'move on.' *What does that mean? How does one simply move on? Was there a manual for this?* My mother often spoke of friends who would slip comments into their conversations to telegraph their disapproval of her lengthy grieving process. I decided to become more careful about what I shared with others.

Fortunately, Debbie ignored the meddler's advice. Over the course of many readings, Debbie channeled various entities. The experience was always exciting, mind-expanding. My late father often dropped by during these sessions. "He keeps saying 'elementals' and something about 'our DNA being triggered,'" Debbie related during one such reading.

"What the heck does that mean?"

"I don't know," she replied.

For the next day or so, I sat with this puzzle. Then an idea dawned on me. I phoned Debbie to explain my hunch. "My dad worked in the field of genetics when he was alive. It's interesting that now he is talking to us about DNA. Is it possible that he's trying to explain that our DNA has the capacity to change or express itself in different ways... maybe energetically?"

"Yes, that could be it," she said on the other end of the line.

"Maybe some people, like you and other mediums, are born with this DNA already triggered?" I suggested. "Maybe the rest of us need a catalyst to ignite our intuitive capabilities. Maybe that's what's happening to me... Aaah!" I screamed and covered my face with my arms as a large hawk flew out of the woods and directly into the window mere feet in front of me. The bird hit the window with such a thud that my son in the basement heard it and asked what the noise was. I was sure it had injured itself, but it flew away as quickly and unexpectedly as it had appeared.

"What happened?" Debbie asked.

"A hawk with a three-foot wingspan just flew right into my window! In the six years I've been living here, I've never seen a hawk in my yard, let alone had one crash into a window. I think it's a pretty clear message that I'm on the right track, eh?"

Debbie wholeheartedly agreed.

I still didn't know what my dad meant by elementals. Debbie

suggested I look up the term on line. I soon after found out that it refers to spirits in nature – within animals, plants, minerals, wind, fire and water. My father had been passionate about the natural world, connecting with it on his walks along the seawall close to my parents' home in Vancouver, British Columbia. He also hiked and skied. Our family and friends called him the Man of the Mountain. Science was his gateway to understanding this passion and uncovering nature's secrets. It made sense that his spirit would connect with us through nature. The combination of the DNA activation discussion and the dramatic sign from nature felt like spiritual poetry to me and an undeniable message from him.

I started writing in a journal as a way to process my grief and document the amazing things I was experiencing. *Who knows,* I thought, *maybe one day I could write a book about all this.* At that time, another guardian angel of sorts came through in a reading with Debbie. It was my great aunt, Amy. I had never met her, but she was my Dad's favorite aunt. Debbie explained that Aunt Amy helps me with my writing. When I asked my mother about her, Mom's tone conveyed love and admiration. "We helped her when she was sick and dying. She had no one else, except for a nurse, ironically named Lianne!"

"That's crazy!" I said. "Was Aunt Amy a writer?"

"Not that I know of."

"Did she have red hair?"

"Yes, flaming red hair. Why?"

"That's how Debbie described her."

"That's amazing! I still have some of her things. Would you

like me to send them to you?"

I replied that I would get them the next time I visited.

I never even met Aunt Amy. Why is she guiding me? And what does her nurse sharing my name mean?

During my next visit to Vancouver, I searched Dad's memorabilia and library. I was surprised to come across a number of works by Mark Twain, Charles Dickens, Edgar Allan Poe, Robert Louis Stevenson and other literary giants. I had never seen him read these novels. I knew him as an avid reader of non-fiction. When I looked at the inside covers, I saw they were all signed: "Love, Aunt Amy." *Maybe she had a strong love or knowledge of literature and that's why she's helping me?* I took the books home and still keep them nearby when I write.

I wanted to find a way to connect directly with my departed loved ones, guides, angels – whoever would communicate with me. I began to meditate regularly. My daily journaling captured my dreams, the many signs/coincidences that I was experiencing, and any impressions or ideas that would come to me. I read books, watched programs, and listened to podcasts to learn all that I could about the non-physical world. I crossed the continent to attend conferences and workshops related to spiritual awakening. I found others like me seeking answers and deeper connections. Some of my friends who had already been such a great support to me wanted to form a small group dedicated to spiritual practice. We were nine women committed to gathering each Monday morning in a Spirit Circle. This group held a safe space for each of us to explore our spiritual beliefs without judgment.

There were also places that felt energetically special or sacred to me, such as Sedona, Arizona. Bob and I had loved the area when we visited it early in our relationship. We had talked about returning one day, but never had the chance. I decided to take the boys there for spring break. I agreed to visit nearby towns and do endless cowboy activities with them in exchange for an afternoon dedicated to what I wanted.

I hired a shaman named Raoul to guide us to the sacred places known as energy vortexes. Kaiden and Kerrsen were not excited about the tour, but went along with it to make good on their promise to me. Raoul had a slight build, long black hair pulled back into a ponytail and the dark brown eyes, sharp nose and high cheekbones of his indigenous lineage. He eagerly shared ancient wisdom and traditions as he pointed out and explained the natural elements on our tour. He then surprised us with a guided visioning exercise at the edge of a remote canyon.

It was late in the day and the sun was casting long shadows on the red rocks. I lay on my back with my feet inches from the cliff's edge. The boys lay next to me. The wind spiraled up through the canyon, creating a haunting echo off the rock walls. I kept my eyes closed as I listened to the soft beat of Raoul's drum. My body felt light, relaxed against the warm rock under me and the cool breeze above. I felt as if I was floating as the tension drained from my body. *This is why I'm in Arizona.* I focused on Raoul's voice rather than worry about what the boys were thinking, whether they were bored, would start to giggle or, worse yet, get up and move too close to the edge.

"Imagine walking alone in the woods," Raoul said, as he beat the drum. "As you walk, notice what you see along the way." I was transported to the circle of trees near my home thousands of miles away. I followed one of the intersecting paths and crossed over a small rickety bridge spanning a bog that I walked over daily with Gunner. The heartbeat rhythm of the drum lulled me into a semi-trance as Raoul began to chant. On the other side of the bog, I saw a fox to the left. Farther along, a doe to my right...

"Continue along your path and, as you do, you will find a cave. Go into that cave. There is someone waiting to give you a gift. Go inside and receive your gift."

My mind left the bright sunshine. Only the dim light of a fire lit my way. Despite the darkness, I knew immediately that Bob was there to greet me. I could feel his warmth radiating throughout the cold damp cave. His smile filled my heart with joy. He stretched out his arm to hand me a miniature pyramid with an engraved eye and said, "Namaste." His single word to me had long been my favorite Sanskrit salutation meaning, "The light in me sees the light in you."

Kee-eeeee-arr. The loud caw of a hawk pierced through my vision, abruptly yanking me back to the cliff's edge.

"What did you see in your vision?" Raoul asked.

I opened my eyes and saw the boys quietly looking at Raoul.

The boys described their experiences first. Kerrsen was intrigued about the meaning behind his vision, but Kaiden was quick to dismiss his experience as just something he remembered seeing on television.

When I detailed my vision, Raoul interpreted the signs for me. The fox represents the afterlife and its presence on my left symbolized my female side and intuition. The fox knows the darkness of the woods intimately, and can be relied upon to guide people in the spirit world. The deer is a sacred carrier of peace and shows us how to open our hearts.

"The gift from your husband is the Eye of Ra," he concluded. "This all-knowing eye represents your third eye, or inner eye. It provides perception beyond normal sight."

I told Raoul that I had lost my glasses at the beginning of our trip – the first time I had ever lost a pair since I had started to wear glasses at the age of 10.

"Sometimes we need to lose our vision in order to really see," he said. "The vividness of the real world, of what we see in front of us is so strong that it distracts us from the subtle language of spirit."

I wondered what else I could see with this new form of seeing.

CHAPTER 13

Into the Mystic

The lights in the room where Bob died kept burning out, one after the other within days of each other. When replacing the bulb didn't work, I tested the sockets. When that failed, I asked a handyman to repair the fixture. "There's nothing wrong with it," he said.

One of the two mechanized garage doors also started acting up. An inch or two from closing, it would abruptly reverse directions, rolling back up. Nothing was blocking the sensors. I checked. Just as mysteriously, the door would close properly when I tried the remote control again. The handyman could never find the cause for this erratic functioning either. These strange kinds of electrical incidents occurred so frequently that I began to wonder if it was Bob trying to communicate with me.

I asked Debbie if she could confirm my suspicion. "Yes, he says it's him," she said after closing her eyes and tuning into Bob's energy.

"Why is he doing this?" I asked a bit frustrated. "It's costing me to try to fix everything."

"He says it's a small price to pay to know that he is still here with you," she replied.

I laughed. "True enough!" Causing havoc with the electrical elements felt like something he would do to get my attention. Even the words she used sounded like him. A few days later, I was in the same room and another light burned out. I was in a hurry and didn't have a lot of patience at that moment for Bob's shenanigans. "Not again, Bob!" I said aloud. "Would you stop doing this? It's getting annoying."

The room was silent. Shame poured over me like a cold shower. "I'm sorry. I know you're just trying to contact me. I do appreciate it. I love knowing that you are still here, but couldn't you make it less work for me?" I laughed at myself as I realized we just had our first inter-dimensional tiff. The next day, when I entered the same room, the light merely flickered and then returned to full power. "That's better. Thank you."

Since Bob seemed eager to connect with me, I decided to take up Debbie's suggestion to communicate with him through automatic writing. I nervously sat down with my journal and pen one evening. I wasn't sure whether anything would come through or if it would all just be my imagination. I tried not to worry, to just have fun. I began by asking questions and then wrote whatever came to mind, without editing.

"Hi, Bob, are you with me right now?" I wrote.

"Yes."

I was surprised at how immediate the response was.

"What are you thinking of?"

"Hallelujah! It can be a bit frustrating trying to get through to people. No one seems to hear me." My hand wrote these words in haste across the paper, seemingly detached from my arm.

"I can imagine. Well, no. I can't really... I miss you."

"I know, but I am here with you. My body may have died, but I am still very much alive."

"Do you miss me as much as I miss you?" I asked.

"It's not the same for me because I can feel your energy."

"What is it like for you?"

"Peaceful. Different... I've been here before. We both have been here, together... a long time ago."

"I wish I could look into your eyes... hear your voice. This reminds me of our long-distance relationship when I lived in Toronto and you were in Montreal. All we had was the phone to connect us and the occasional email. We longed to be together all the time. When it finally happened, we kind of took it for granted, didn't we? I swear if you were here with me again I would never take it for granted. I would hold onto you and never let you go."

"But you know that's not the way the Universe works. Everything is impermanent. One day, when we are both in spirit, we will look back at this time and wish we had cherished it more. It is truly an amazing time for us – to be communicating like this."

"But how do I know it is not all in my head... that I am not just making this up? I think and feel it's real, but I wonder if I am just soothing the pain."

For a moment, I couldn't hear anything. "Bob, are you still

there?"

"Yes, that's what happens with doubt. It cuts off the connection. You feel the truth deep within you. Messages come spontaneously, ideas that were not previously available to your conscious mind pop into your head."

I was amazed by this new process and all the revelations I was experiencing. It was as if I was downloading valuable files from the ether. Somehow I could feel Bob's excitement as I translated the thoughts into words. He explained that his death was the catalyst for my awakening. He was eager to let me know that the way we were communicating between physical and non-physical was special. We had tried to do this for millennia in different lifetimes, but we had always fallen short. The timing wasn't right. The beliefs of our cultures and societies in those lifetimes didn't support us. I felt such gratitude for this new channel to Bob. Like an eager journalist on the brink of a ground-breaking story, I continued to delve further into the mysteries of death and the afterlife.

"Can you explain to me more of what it is like where you are?"

"Well, it feels light, much lighter than when I had a body. It feels lighter emotionally and physically."

"Do you miss the five senses?"

"Sometimes, but there is such calm and peace. The other lightness relates to not being bound by time or space. I can see and move into past, future and present moments effortlessly. I can also move wherever I want just by thinking about it. I can sense vibrations, and so can you. Vibrations are emitted by everything – thoughts, feelings, things. Your eyes, ears and skin are tuned to perceive the lower vibrations, but there are higher, more subtle vibrations that you can tune into, if you focus."

"Do you miss living on Earth?"

"I assume you mean with you in my previous incarnation as Bob? There are infinite parts of me, of you, and of everyone, in different dimensions and timelines – past, present and future. To answer your question, I miss being with you, sitting where you are sitting right now, feeling the wind blow against my skin, smelling the summer air, hearing the lawn mower in the distance. That is why it's important not to become so lost in the tasks of earthly life that you miss these moments."

Then I dared to ask the biggest question that I had been pondering since his death. "What was it like to die?"

"The last days and hours in my human form were scary and confusing for me. It was kind of like a dream state. I wasn't sure if I was awake or asleep most of the time. My conscious mind was not registering what was happening. I was convinced I somehow could still fight the cancer that was consuming my body. 'Things are happening too fast,' I kept saying to you. And they were. You gathered the family quickly. The last day I remember people talking, but I felt detached, floating above the conversation, above the room. I could feel each person's emotions. I could sense the fear, sadness, compassion and confusion. I had a sense of another realm as well. It was like being half-asleep and half-awake. I was in neither state, but conscious of both. Loud sounds would pull me back down into my body. Yet I was excited to see where I was going next. The more time I spent there, the less I wanted to come back. When I did, the emotions in the room held me almost like a vice-grip. I couldn't breathe, literally or figuratively. I felt trapped.

"At night, while everyone slept, I was able to spend more time in the other realm with fewer interruptions. I started to feel more grounded there, and less so in the physical world. I could have left then, but my body hung on. When I woke in the middle of the night, you were there sitting with me. You took off my wedding ring, because my hand was getting too swollen to wear it comfortably. You asked me if I knew what was written inside. I said, 'Love will keep us alive.' Then I tried to say that I wished I had focused more of my time and energy on just loving and being loved. All I could get out was, 'More love.'"

"Yes, I remember. I thought you were trying to tell me that I should be more patient with you, because it was so hard for me to be your caregiver. I felt bad about this for such a long time after you died."

"I know and I am sorry about that, but I was trying to relay the message to you to focus on love and all would be okay. I wanted you to know that our love would continue. It wasn't ending with the death of my body. I could see that then.

"Remember when you took me from my bed and by wheelchair into the family room. Together we watched the last sunrise of my life. It was spectacular, maybe the best one ever. The dawn light reflected on the golden and burnt orange leaves of the maple trees in the backyard. I don't know how I knew this, because as you know, I was colorblind. The gray clouds and moody mist reflected the bittersweet contrast in the emotions I was feeling about the departure I was about to make.

"You asked me to describe what I saw. I told you colors, but it was much more than the colors outside. I saw a beautiful glow of orange emanating from you and behind you. I understood that I had chosen the timing of my departure and it was part of a larger plan. The orange of the season matched the vibration of our twin flame energy. I knew at that moment that this would be an important clue that would help you to figure things out. I could see how everything was interconnected – time, seasons, life events, emotions and so much more. They are the breadcrumbs that are revealed to those who are open to seeing them.

"The time of my death, 2:11 p.m., 2+1+1=4, on the 4th of October was another part of this grand scheme. I could also see that the time of year, autumn, would strike a deep chord within you, because we were married in the fall. As the months became colder, I knew you would use the restorative essence of the season to retreat and heal. I was confident that you would come out in the spring much stronger.

"As I lay in bed waiting to transcend, my older children and brothers came to say goodbye. They didn't know that I could hear them. I could also feel their emotions, but I couldn't respond. This was tremendously hard. The love we shared and the sadness of the separation was a crushing weight on my heart. I so wanted to reach out and comfort each one, to tell them I was going to be all right, that this wasn't the end. As the time came to leave, it was easier when my closest loved ones, you and my children, weren't by my side. You whispered in my ear that it was okay for me to leave and that you and the boys would be okay. That comforted me and gave me a sense of peace. I know it was hard not being in the room when I died, but your presence kept me grounded in my body. So I found a time when you weren't there. Our boys were on their way home, my girls were at the store, and Kevin and you were out of the room. That is when I sneaked out, like a thief in the night.

"When you entered into the room a moment later, Bruce Cockburn's *Waiting for a Miracle* was playing. The song was another breadcrumb. The lyrics described the miracle of death at that point, when the angel within us is set free. As I left my body, I experienced a brilliant multicolored light wrapping around me and lifting me out of my body. I was immediately greeted by a spirit. He appeared as a man, thin with a gray and white beard. He was of northern European origins. He was my transition guide. I saw my father, too. He greeted me with, 'Good to see you, son.' I felt the warmth and love coming from him. It was familiar and comforting. There were others I recognized on a heart level, but I didn't know in this life.

"It then came time to review my life. I was scared, because I had lived with so much guilt. I saw how the things I did and worried so much about, like my divorce, were really part of a greater plan. I understood that my guilt and shame were wasteful and destructive energies. I also saw, or rather felt, the joy I brought to people's lives – to you, my mother, my brothers, my children and friends. It took my breath away, or at least it felt that way. It really surprised me. For so much of my life, I felt unworthy. Now I realized how poorly I had interpreted what others thought of me. Seeing other lifetimes and this broader perspective even helped me to see the positive impact my death would have on you and my children."

My pen kept moving non-stop. I was amazed at how clearly the sentences flowed onto the page. Effortlessly, all of these thoughts and sentiments popped into my head. In many cases they were ideas that I had never considered, yet they felt so authentic. The process felt like a flow of inspiration working through me rather than by me. It made me feel closer to Bob in a way that I never did when he was alive. We shared thoughts almost like one consciousness rather than two minds. I continued to ask him for more details about his last moments. Then I thanked him for explaining why he chose to die when I wasn't in the room and for helping me to understand everything better. I still didn't comprehend what he meant by 'twin flames' and asked him to explain.

"You used to refer to us as soulmates. This is not exactly correct. The term soulmate refers to when two souls come together to teach one another or to work out grievances from past lives. A twin flame is a bit different. Soulmates are like siblings and some are even like fraternal twins, while twin flames are like identical twins. As with identical twins, they originate as one cell or higher soul and split apart to create two individuals. They are the negative and positive, the male and female of a whole. They are connected through a strong bond of love. Just as identical twins have a bond that goes beyond their physical resemblance, the same is true for twin flames. It's like the Phil Collins song, *Two Hearts* but one mind.

"The purpose of twin flames coming together in a lifetime is not so much to work out past karma – although there may be some of that, too. It is more to co-create and, more specifically, to co-evolve. Imagine the power of two halves coming together to create as a whole. Twin flames don't always live on Earth at the same time. There are an unprecedented number of twin flames incarnating at this critical time, when the planet and all that lives upon her are ascending. It is this powerful creative force of the twin flame energy that can help make significant leaps forward for individuals, as well as for the collective.

"As you know from our experience, when twin flames incarnate at the same time, there is a fierce connection between them that is impossible to deny. This can be said for soulmates as well, but the attraction of twin flames is even more powerful, like two massive magnets. If they are alive at the same time, hell or high water can't keep them apart. While some connect with their twin flame in physical form, others are guided and supported by their non-physical twin flame.

"Just as we have a blueprint of our physical and energetic makeup in our DNA, we also have a life blueprint before we incarnate. Of course there is free will and choice, so nothing is set in stone. However, our life's purpose is clearly outlined, the players chosen, and the stage set. How much we ad lib versus keeping to the script is up to us. When twin flames decide to incarnate, the main purpose is to help each other ascend. Ascension doesn't mean going to some remote place called heaven, but rather to embody spirit and consciously awaken to a greater extent while in physical form. It works the other way as well. While I am working with you on your ascension, you are also helping me. As your twin flame, I advance spiritually through your experience, and vice versa. We are ascending together. So my death was not some act of chivalry, but rather a mutually beneficial process."

I was overwhelmed by all of this radical insight. I needed to take a break to process everything. Before I stopped writing, however, I wanted to understand what Bob had described as the connection between the orange of the season and the vibration of our twin flame energy.

"Light, colors, sound... they are all vibrations with a resonance. Twin flames are two souls that vibrate at the same frequency, like two radios tuned into one station. You and I resonate to the same frequency within the orange spectrum. This is in tune with the second chakra – the energy center of your body that is responsible for creativity, relationships and, of course, sex. So, our co-creative purpose revolves around these areas."

"This is so incredible, Bob. I am learning so much. I can't believe how easy it is to tap into this wisdom and information."

"That's the thing, Lianne. It has been hidden for thousands of years. This is knowledge that only the most devout individuals and members of secret societies knew and shared among themselves... Until now, when it is available to everyone. You can show others how they, too, can tap into their own well of knowledge, like you are beginning to do. You don't need extraordinary abilities... just desire and focus."

I started wondering if my dad's message about triggering DNA had anything to do with what Bob was saying about this hidden knowledge now available to all of us. A few days later, I decided to try to connect with my father through an automatic writing session.

I began as I did with Bob by writing a greeting. "Hi, Dad... Are you there?"

"Of course!" I heard his distinct voice in my head.

"Wow, this is cool! I have had so many dreams with you lately. How are you?"

"I'm fine. That was me trying to get your attention."

I noticed there was a different tone and feeling in this session compared to the one with Bob. My dad was matter-of-fact, whereas Bob felt more loving.

"Mom is doing much better, now that she feels she can connect with you," I told him. My mother's readings with Debbie had lifted her spirits. Some of the information that came through was so accurate and specific that my mother shifted from not believing in any afterlife to trying to communicate with my father on a regular basis.

"Yes, thank you for helping her with that," came his response to me.

"I'm still wondering about the message that you were trying to get across to Debbie and me about 'triggering DNA.' Can you explain that to me?"

"Yes, this is a very interesting time indeed. The Earth and all life on it are shifting. Many people call it *awakening*. It is an ever-evolving consciousness and your DNA is the key to unlocking this process. Just as your body evolves, so does your energetic body."

"How does this work?"

"Your thoughts create feelings in your heart which then produces electromagnetic energy that stimulates the body's systems – hormones, adrenals, electrical, fight or flight responses, etcetera. This all switches specific key-codes of light in your DNA either on or off. The more of these key-codes that are switched on, the higher the vibration; a lot of key-codes switched 'off' equals a low vibration or denser energy."

"What is the difference between low and high vibration?"

"There is a lot of difference, but let me start by saying that high vibration relates to a feeling of harmony, oneness and ease of manifestation. Low vibration gives us a sense of separateness, dis-ease and a sluggish movement through space and time, which is typical of your third dimension or physical reality.

"You're aware of the two strands of physical DNA, but there are actually twelve strands in total. The additional ten strands are dormant in most humans at this time, but are slowly being activated. When they become activated, they broaden your perspective of awareness and level of consciousness. Hence the idea of *awakening*. Fully activated DNA is an orchestra that has a repertoire to draw upon with many musicians playing a variety of instruments. By contrast, a limited DNA activation is like a small band that plays just one genre of music – say, country – and has a shorter playlist. The band attracts only people who like country and may even repel those who do not. However, the large orchestra has the ability to play every kind of music and attract all types of people. It is a metaphor for a true collective or oneness. The combination of key-codes and activated DNA are the connection here. The more DNA that is activated, the more connected one feels to all things. The more that remains dormant, the more separate and alone one feels."

"Why do negative thoughts and feelings turn off these switches or key-codes of light, while positive ones turn them on?" I asked.

"It relates to the law of polarity. It is simply a spectrum. It is like saying why is black dark and white light... It is the polarity that is associated with each of them. Negative thoughts of fear, guilt and shame have a low frequency, while positive ones consisting of compassion, appreciation and love are higher. Here is the equation in simple terms:

- Thoughts influence feelings.
- Feelings influence the body's electromagnetic and chemical physical reaction.
- The physical reaction turns DNA key-codes of light on or off.
- Key-codes of light raise or lower the vibration of a being.
- The level of vibration creates the sense of oneness or separateness.

We control our thoughts and, therefore, our reality. Meditation, art, prayer, work we love, relaxation, music, dance and more all help us to influence our thoughts and feelings in a positive way. We can also stimulate this DNA activation directly through our heart, via love of all kinds, and through our body with physical exercise, certain food and drink. And that's how we can alter our thought process."

"Incredible! Does this relate to how Bob developed cancer?"

"Yes, Bob's father had traces of asbestos on his coat from the factory where he worked. When Bob was a boy, he inhaled some of these fibers by greeting his dad with a hug. The fibers lay dormant in his body for decades. They may have remained that way if Bob hadn't developed such guilt about leaving his wife and children to be with you. The lower vibrations triggered by these negative feelings about himself caused a cascade of physical reactions that allowed the cancer to develop and eventually spread."

My father's explanation about Bob's illness made sense to me. I was amazed at the flow of information that was coming through almost effortlessly. I wasn't sure I understood everything my father communicated to me, but I felt the truth and importance of his message. I searched the Internet for more information, but there was very little available at the time about the twelve-strand DNA activation. Now there are numerous online articles, videos and blog posts. What I did manage to find back then further confirmed for me that I was not making this stuff up, but accessing deep wisdom from the spirit realm. I sensed my new abilities to connect with Bob and now my father were directly related to what Dad was saying about our world awakening by activating our energetic DNA.

CHAPTER 14
Lyin' Eyes

He was a work acquaintance. I offered him advice to help build his business. His wife was present the few times we met. I became friends with her as well and asked them both to participate in an event I was organizing. A month before the event, she canceled without explanation. When I ran into her, she responded to my friendly chatter with single-word responses. I asked what was wrong, but she brushed me off. A couple of days later, she phoned.

"As a life coach, I know how important it is to speak our truth," she began. "I advise clients to do the same. So I must tell you that I am not comfortable with the way you are acting towards my husband. You need to back off and create some healthy boundaries. I don't want this to hurt your relationship with him, because I know he respects you. I just had to tell you how I was feeling."

I sat dumbfounded on the other end of the line. "What are you talking about?" My mind raced to recall something I had done that could have been misinterpreted.

"When I see the way you look at him, it makes me physically sick," she continued. "I want to throw up."

I wondered if she had lost her sanity, or had phoned the wrong number. I had no interest in her husband. He was simply a work-related collaborator and friend. I felt like a child being reprimanded for something I hadn't done.

The next day I approached her husband after yoga class to see if there was something happening between them that had caused her to react to me the way that she had.

"No, this has nothing to do with me," he stated with cool indifference. "This issue is strictly between her and you." The way he brushed me off, seemingly placing at least some of the blame on me, confounded me. I turned my anger inwards. *What have you done, Lianne? Did you smile too much, talk too much, laugh too loud?* I interrogated myself, but I couldn't think of anything.

I consulted Don, a long-time business partner and good friend. "Don, has your wife ever been jealous of me or said that I've acted inappropriately?"

He laughed. "Of course not!"

I let out a huge sigh.

"Lianne, this has nothing to do with you," he insisted. "This is obviously their issue, which they're projecting onto you. Don't let it get to you."

Too late. I couldn't shake my seeming lack of outer awareness. I had been doing so much personal and spiritual development that I mistakenly thought I was beyond everyday drama.

Long suppressed feelings about my affair with Bob resurfaced. The guilt I had felt about being the scandalous other woman re-emerged. I didn't understand why this was coming up again. I thought I had dealt with those conflicted feelings a long time ago. Apparently not. I asked Bob to help me work through these feelings again by my posing questions to him and writing down the first thoughts or images that popped into my head.

I started off grumbling to Bob that I hadn't realized how much I was still affected by the guilt linked with the start of our relationship. "Bob, I saw you struggle with the guilt for so many years, but I didn't realize it was my problem, too," I wrote.

"It was *our* problem that we never spoke about – probably because it was too painful," I added. "I thought discussing it would bring up bad feelings and jinx our life. Not talking about it seems to have done exactly that."

"Don't be so hard on yourself," Bob's soothing voice said deep inside my head. "I never wanted to go there with you either. You encouraged me to get help from therapists, but I didn't believe I had the right to feel better. I thought I deserved to suffer."

My heart felt heavy as I remembered the countless times, especially in the early phase of our relationship, that I tried to convince Bob that he deserved to be happy. "But I don't understand why this situation with this guy and his wife is bothering me so much," I wrote.

"It's bringing up unresolved guilt. Like an undigested meal, it keeps repeating on you. It is true that the issue between him and his wife has nothing to do with you. The same was true in my case. My ex-wife and I had grown apart. The reasons were many, but the result was the same: a relationship that no longer served either of us. I longed to be free, to grow, and to be totally cherished by another. You came into my life and offered me all this… exactly when I needed it. But you weren't responsible for breaking up my marriage. You were an innocent bystander who was swept up in the collateral damage."

I welcomed this new perspective. I had never thought of these key relationships in this way, but his explanation resonated with me.

"Do you remember how I used to say that most romantic relationships start out being amazing, with lots of passion and love, but over time become ordinary?" he asked.

"Yes, I remember you saying that many times in our early years together. Later, we used to ask each other from time to time: 'Have we become ordinary yet?' and then laugh at the absurdity of this idea. Our relationship was a lot of things, but it was far from ordinary."

"Before meeting you, I believed that all relationships eventually became ordinary. When you fall in love, it is akin to your soul being seen by another. That is the essence of the ancient term Namaste. It means: the light in me sees the light in you. It is acknowledgement that we have been seen for whom we really are. It feels amazing, so wonderful that we don't want to lose this feeling. So, we try to control it. This is the path of unconditional love moving into conditional love: I will continue to love you if you adhere to my terms. We were lucky: we rarely let our individual fears of separation layer our love with conditions. So it remained and continues to remain pure. One example of this was when I was dying and you encouraged me to seek alternative healing options. You were terrified of losing me and wanted me to do whatever it took to save myself."

I nodded. "Yes, I remember the way you tenderly looked at me and said with so much love and compassion, 'Lianne, this may be your way, but it's not mine.' Your words and the way you said them pierced through my suffocating fear of losing you to hear what you really needed in that moment." I hadn't seen this from his perspective earlier. At the time, I just knew I couldn't push him anymore. He was doing his best.

"Yes, I was trying to tell you that I had to leave. I had made the decision on a soul level, even though I wasn't conscious of it at the time. Instead of railing against me, you accepted my wishes gracefully. I think I felt more love for you in that moment than I ever had. It has been said that when you love another, you must set that person free. This is the highest demonstration of unconditional love, yet the most difficult. I know that if you had been given the chance, you would have exchanged places with me. You would have given up your life for mine. Your path was actually the harder one. My pain and suffering ended, but yours intensified with my death. This is the first lifetime in which you are starting to master conscious awareness and unconditional love," he offered.

So much was swirling through my head — new awareness, more questions. I felt my entire being vibrate with excitement. My experience of connecting with Bob was more delicious than a hot fudge sundae on a gorgeous summer day! I wanted more.

I especially wanted to understand what he meant by "the first lifetime." Had we shared other lifetimes? Over the next few weeks, I kept a journal of my dreams. I also continued my automatic writing exchanges with Bob. During my long walks in nature, I sat quietly to hear any messages that I might receive from spirit. I read books to develop skills to connect with intuition and to do past-life regression on my own. The following is a summarized account of what I saw and experienced in dreams, meditative and hypnotic-like states over the course of many weeks – all of which I documented in my journal.

Bob and I were seated in a double chairlift that was flying hundreds of feet above the ground. We were soaring over a city. I couldn't hear, smell or feel anything. It was strange, because I didn't miss any of these senses. Their absence made me feel completely at peace, almost like relaxing in a sensory deprivation tank. I was amazed at how special this was, how calm I felt.

As we landed, I noted the swiftness of our transportation. It seemed as if we had traveled half way around the world in an instant. We were in a station of sorts, with many doors and people coming and going. I noticed a long wall of doors with dates. The years 1914 and 1944 stood out for me. I looked back at Bob. He appeared happy and healthy – the way he was before he became sick. "Where and what is this place?" I asked.

"A transfer station in the non-physical realm. Pretty cool, eh? You don't feel anything with your senses because there are no senses here – just seeing and knowing. The transfer station is the place between lives. The numbers are important dates in previous lifetimes. Notice the fours: 1914 and 1944. Let's go check it out."

The chairlift started to move again with my feet dangling below me. We went through the 1944 door. Once inside, a giant screen appeared in front of us. A band of young soldiers showed up on the screen. They looked British. They stood on a hilltop overlooking a desert in what appeared to be North Africa. The young men in their late teens or early twenties stood around smoking and teasing each other. I suddenly went from merely watching the scene unfold on the screen to experiencing it as one of the young men. I was not quite in his body, but rather hovering just behind it. I was still mostly a detached observer within this perspective, but able to experience senses and emotions.

A deep fondness and love washed over me as I next experienced this same body turn towards a car parked next to us. I opened the door of the red 1940s Oldsmobile and slid across the front leathered bench-seating toward the passenger side. My battalion leader, whose name I somehow knew to be Nick, sat beside me. An explosion of bullets suddenly pierced the car's frame, windows, and my body. Nick tried to shield me with his body, but it was too late. When the surprise enemy attack ended, Nick pulled me out of the car onto the dusty ground. He cradled my head in his lap. "You're going to be all right. Everything is going to be all right." His tears betrayed his words.

I felt myself lift out of my body and float above everyone. My comrades encircled my body and stared down at it. I recognized some of the men from my current lifetime. One was my son, Kerrsen. Another was my oldest, closest friend, Tom. And, the battalion leader, Nick, was Bob. The whole scene was surreal. I was gripped by a powerful sense of attachment. I didn't want to leave these men. I loved them. I could tell they didn't want to lose me either.

My spirit or consciousness drifted farther up and away from them. When I turned around, I was greeted by an old friend – a mentor I hadn't seen for centuries. "It's you, Master!" I said with elation. "Have you been with me all of this time?"

"Yes, indeed, my son, I have always been here. This was a very difficult lifetime for you. It was short, but full of cruelty – by you and by others towards you. Now is your time to rest and cleanse the hurt, pain and shame," he said compassionately as he led me to a massive waterfall surrounded by a magnificent forest. I could feel the cooling mist on my face, while lush green scents entered my nose, and a cacophony of birds and other animals filled my ears. Then I found myself next to Bob on the chairlift again.

"Are you ready to see another lifetime?" he asked encouragingly. We exited the 1944 room and entered 1914 through a great hall. A rural landscape somewhere in England appeared on the big screen. This time I inhabited the body of a woman in her mid-thirties lying on a four-poster bed inside a small cottage. White ruffled sheets and a homemade quilt covered my sickly body. A fire crackled in the hearth across the room, even though it was August. The sun was shining through the window adjacent to my bed, reflecting off the golden hair of a little boy who sat next to me. He knew something bad was happening to his mother. I was dying, but held onto the remaining scrap of life within me because I was terrified of leaving him behind.

"Nicholas, you will be okay," I tried to reassure him, and myself. I couldn't look at him, fearing my eyes would betray the anxiety I felt inside. My sister had agreed to help my boy's father to look after him, but I feared he wouldn't receive the attention he needed. I wanted him to continue to be loved and cherished the way I had been raising him.

As I watched all of this unfold, I sensed the connection between this life and the one I had just witnessed in the 1944 room. This little boy, Nicholas, would grow up to become, Nick – my battalion leader in North Africa. I was astonished to realize that Bob had experienced a lifetime as Nicholas/Nick, while I had lived first as his mother who had died when he was very young, and then as his charge in World War II some thirty years later. I was amazed at the vast interconnectedness being revealed to me.

I sat back on the chairlift in awe. I asked Bob to show me a lifetime that most related to my current situation and that might help me overcome the loss I was feeling. Bob pointed to the 1852 room. As we entered, the screen depicted a Georgian mansion in Louisiana. The scene came to life with such clarity — images, sounds, emotions and precise names, dates and places — as if I was reliving the experience.

On the second storey, a young brunette sat in her boudoir readying for the party already taking place a floor below. Once again I became the character on the screen. I looked into the mirror and a pretty face stared back at me. What struck me the most was the deceit in my eyes.

I heard a commotion downstairs. An uninvited individual had

arrived at the door. Intuitively I knew it was George. He was a man I loved deeply, but the son of a poor farmer. I had chosen to marry another man for wealth and social status instead. Shortly into the marriage, I realized my mistake. Over the past several months, George and I had been meeting in secret. I had promised to leave my husband, but doubted I would have the courage. I couldn't tell George this truth. I feared losing my only happiness.

My stomach knotted. *Why is he here? What is he going to say?*

"What are you doing here?" my husband Billy asked, knowing a bit about my childhood relationship with George.

"I am here for Martha," George replied, obviously bolstered by liquor.

"What on God's Earth are you talking about?" Billy demanded.

"Martha loves me. She should have never married you. She's planning to leave you to live with me."

Everyone hushed for Billy's response.

Billy gave a dismissive chuckle. "Oh, does she? And, how do you know this?"

"She told me," George replied. "Every Saturday night, when you leave her to gallivant around town with your whores, she comes to me to get the love and tenderness that you neglect to give her."

"How dare you, sir!" Billy shouted. "How dare you talk about me or my wife like that in my house, in front of my friends?"

"Why don't you ask her yourself?"

I had remained upstairs, like a scared mouse, barely able to breathe. The moment of truth had finally come. I had to make a decision. I couldn't avoid it anymore. *Do I choose love and risk being ostracized by my community, even possibly inviting physical harm to George or me? Or do I stay in a loveless relationship with a man who can at least take care of me?* I wished I had the courage to follow my heart, but I was fairly sure I didn't. I hated myself for my cowardice.

As I made my way down the curved staircase, I felt all eyes on me. Billy stared at me with his brow furrowed. I sensed he still thought I was a victim of this whole unfortunate incident. If I had any previous doubts, I now knew what I had to do.

"Martha, George here has quite a story," Billy said as I reached the ground level. "He says you love him, that you have been meeting in secret and you intend to leave me for him. Is this true?"

I took a deep breath.

George looked at me in anticipation. Billy glared at me, his eyes demanding an answer.

"No, Billy, that is not true," I lied.

A collective sigh filled the room.

"What are you talking about, Martha?" George said almost choking. "Tell him the truth. Tell him that we are in love and always have been. Tell him that you are going to leave him and that we have plans for a life together."

I felt bile rise in my throat. I swallowed hard. "While it is true that George and I may have had a childish infatuation for each other when we were younger, that is long over. Billy, I have no intention of leaving you."

I tried to avoid the shock on George's face, but I couldn't. His eyes locked onto mine, pleading me to tell the truth. My mind flashed back to a few years earlier when George had intercepted the horses and carriage taking me to marry Billy. George had looked so devastated as he stood with a bouquet of frangipanis for me. Now, surrounded by others, his face again filled with so much hurt from my newest betrayal that my heart felt scorched by his pain. Shame permeated every fiber of my being. I wanted to run and hide, but my legs would not move.

As I watched the screen from the safety of the flying chairlift again, my teeth clenched and my body tensed as I braced myself for what I knew would come next. Bob glanced at me, asking if I was certain that I wanted to continue. I nodded.

I turned back towards the screen. Billy was provoking the guests to teach George a lesson for defaming his wife and his good name. They immediately encircled George and dragged him outside. Martha screamed at them to leave George alone, as one of the guests restrained her.

While I couldn't see what was happening outside, I could hear everything. One man yelled for a rope, another for a ladder, as George pleaded to be set free. The blood in my veins turned to ice. "No," Martha screamed. "Don't hurt him! What he said is true. He wasn't lying. I take it all back. Don't hurt him."

It was too late. My cries were muffled by the jeering of the angry mob. No mercy was extended to George who fell victim to Southern justice from an oak tree. Martha stood catatonic as the crowd returned to the mansion, cheering and laughing.

Billy entered with an air of righteousness. "You won't have to worry about him bothering us anymore."

"I will never forgive you for this, Billy." Martha spat with a hatred that was really meant for herself.

I sat back on the chairlift, sobbing as I relived the anguish. The images fast-forwarded. As the years flashed by, I could see that I never forgave myself. I recoiled from life, torturing myself with self-recrimination. I missed George terribly. I would dream of him, hear his voice in my head, and occasionally sensed what could have been his spirit's presence, but my guilty conscious wouldn't let him closer. In the end, I died of consumption. My corrosive emotions literally consumed me from the inside out. I again experienced my own death. My soul detached from my body in an upward swoosh. I was immediately greeted by George – Bob's spirit. Our reconnection was sublime, immediately lifting the guilt that I had endured for so long.

I looked away from the screen at Bob quietly sitting next to me. "So these are the famous George and Martha?"

"Yes, we had a strong soul connection throughout many lives and even between lifetimes. I've only shown you a few. When two people who've had such a connection in a previous lifetime kiss or touch for the first time, there is an exchange, a soul knowing. There is a small opening in the thick veil that separates dimensions to reveal a sense of their past lives. This is what happened when we kissed for the first time outside the restaurant that night. Martha and George were nudging us to wake up."

"I guess losing you in this lifetime was karma for causing your death in that one."

"No, karma is not like that. It's not a punishment. It represents the soul's desire to experience and express all aspects of itself.

It's not like an obligation to pay a debt, but an opportunity to experience the effects of decisions and actions taken during another lifetime. The purpose of life is to evolve into whole beings who are aware of all aspects of themselves and can shape their light consciously."

"I've noticed things that I think are linked to previous lifetimes, clues to connect me back to those experiences. The song by the Eagles, *Lyin' Eyes,* always affected me in a peculiar way. Whenever I heard it, I felt a deep sense of remorse, without knowing why. I now understand that the lyrics relate a story similar to my own experiences in that past life."

"Yes!" Bob replied eagerly. "A strong reaction, positive or negative, to people, places, songs, movies, or even flowers, like frangipanis, are like threads connecting us to other lifetimes. Seeing them triggers an unconscious knowing within us."

"I see now the frangipanis were an example of that! When we were married in Bali, they were everywhere, including on our bed and in the pool in our villa next to where we took our first dance. We were enamoured by the beauty, simplicity and scent of the flower. When we returned to Canada, we were quite disappointed to find the flower didn't exist in our colder climate. Now I see how that flower was symbolic on a soul level. As George, you had offered me, then Martha, a bouquet of frangipanis when you tried to persuade me to marry you instead of Billy. It's like the Universe had a sense of humor placing them all around us when finally we were married."

"Ah, you see humor is divine!" Bob said, laughing.

I now understood how life truly is but a stage, that our souls agree to play different roles to offer us important lessons and experiences. Bob and I shared love and loss in many different ways over many lifetimes. Our love never died with the death of our bodies.

As a result, I started to see the people who I felt had wronged me in a different light. I realized that the so-called villains in my life actually had difficult roles. My anger towards the work friend and his wife transformed into compassion and, eventually, gratitude. They had sparked the dream that led me to release an emotional block I had unconsciously held for years, maybe even lifetimes. I felt a great sense of relief. I started to wonder what other unconscious crap I was still carrying.

CHAPTER 15
Painter Song

I lay on the family room couch waiting for a friend to arrive so we could go out for dinner. The familiar sounds of the clock ticking in the next room, the furnace air blowing, and my young children giggling upstairs with the babysitter lulled me into a semi-sleep. In the distance, I heard the whistle of the daily commuter train approaching. It reminded me of a typical day when Bob was still healthy. I arrived home at the end of a long commute from the city to the appetizing aroma of meatloaf on the stove. My sons ran to the front door with outstretched arms to greet me. Bob's smile and warm hug welcomed me as I entered the kitchen. The stress of the long commute and tough workday melted away. Dinner was already on the table. We sat down and shared our stories of the day as we ate.

The second whistle jolted me back to reality. I braced myself for the wave of grief that normally washed over me after such a sweet memory. Instead, I was surprised to feel a slight sense of relief. I was happy that at least I no longer had to commute hours daily to work. I ran a strategy consulting business for the ten years since I moved to Montreal to marry Bob. I enjoyed the work, but also found it stressful. While I took pride in helping my clients to realize their vision for their organizations and brands, I was still left feeling empty. I missed having a socially larger purpose to my work, like I had in Toronto working for an international development agency years earlier.

I had stopped taking clients during Bob's final months. After Bob died, I didn't have anywhere I had to be or anything I had to do for the first time for as long as I could remember. I had no partner, and no work. After months of exploring realms of consciousness and spirituality, I realized I did not want to return to my consulting business or the kind of marketing jobs I had done earlier. With my children still young enough to adapt to whatever I decided, I was completely free to do whatever I wanted next. Like a painter in front of a blank canvas, I felt both excitement and anxiousness. *Where do I start? What colors do I choose? What should I create? What is best for the boys and me and our future?*

I loved to travel. It had been a dream of mine to live and work abroad. Bali was sacred to me – my mecca, where Bob and I married. The island is like a living temple with the most exquisite natural beauty. Lush jungles, tiered rice fields, active volcanic peaks, pristine beaches all serve as backdrop for stunning Balinese architecture. Simple thatch-roof homes contrast the complex Hindu temples comprised of multiple levels and pavilions. The Balinese are lovely, peaceful and spiritual people. Their culture is rich in tradition, faith and creativity. The nation's cultural center, Ubud, is like an artist's utopia. Miles and miles of streets brim with stores selling every type of art, craft and artisanal creation imaginable. This vibrant place with its deep spirituality offered great inspiration for my blank canvas.

A friend had serendipitously sent me some information about a new type of school that had recently opened in Bali — the first of its kind by having zero ecological impact. The school's philosophy focused on children learning from their own experiences rather than presented theories. I promptly contacted the school and planned a visit with the boys to investigate the idea of living in Bali for a year or two. I was so excited. The prospect of a new and exotic adventure was thrilling. I knew that a return to Bali would be healing for me as well.

As we settled into the thirty-six-hour journey to Bali, I was nervous about taking my young children such a long way on my own. I noticed that the plane was full except for the aisle seat right next to me. This was our first flight without Bob. I smiled and pointed to the seat. "Look, Daddy is with us! He even reserved a seat for himself." Kerrsen laughed and nodded, but Kaiden rolled his eyes.

"Mom, I am a man of science," Kaiden said. "I don't believe in spiritual stuff."

A little while later, Kaiden told me to look outside. Immediately beyond his window was a small circular rainbow, about a foot in diameter, encircling the plane's right wing. I had never seen anything like it.

"You still think this spiritual stuff is hogwash?" I asked.

He remained silent.

Throughout the flight, Bob seemed to have an influence on the songs that randomly played on my iPhone. It was as if Bob's spirit was reassuring me that he was with us and everything would be okay.

I wanted to spread Bob's ashes off the cliff where we had married. I wasn't sure whether the airline permitted a person's remains on board, so I decided not to mention the small glass container in my luggage, although I worried about getting caught breaking a rule. When finally we disembarked in Bali, I noticed a man holding a sign with my name on it. My heart jumped. He took me aside and said: "Problem with bag! Must go to counter."

"What is the problem?" I asked, trying to steady my voice.

"Must go to JAL," he replied, pointing to the Japan Airlines counter.

As we approached the customs wickets, Kaiden pointed to large signs that read: Death penalty for drug trafficking. "Isn't that a bit harsh?" he said with wisdom beyond his ten years.

Oh, my God. What if the customs officers think the ashes are some sort of drug and they take me away for questioning? I started to sweat, imagining myself being separated from the boys. I tried to calm myself. Once through customs, I anxiously made my way to the service counter. The agent greeted me with a smile. "Ah, Miss Bridges, very sorry. Your bag missing. Still in Chicago. It be here tomorrow. We give you fifty dollars for your inconvenience."

I wanted to reach across the counter to kiss the agent. "Thank you, thank you, thank you." I don't think the agent ever saw anyone so elated at having delayed luggage. On the cab ride to our hotel, I smiled at the irony of Bob's ashes being stuck in Chicago. Perhaps it was his way of reassuring us that his presence no longer relied on any kind of physical essence.

The next day, my bag arrived without incident. We drove to the Four Seasons resort in Bali where Bob and I were married twelve years earlier. Armed guards met our car. A thorough search with a bomb-sniffing dog made it clear this was no longer the peaceful Shangri-La that I remembered. The hotel was adjacent to the beach resort bombed in a series of terrorist attacks five years earlier. After the car inspection, the guards ushered us past large wrought-iron gates into our resort complex.

"Welcome to the Four Seasons," the bellhop said in a pleasant voice. "How may I help you today?"

"We have a reservation at the Beach Café," I said as I struggled to hold back tears. "I'm sorry. I'm a little emotional because this is where my husband – their father – and I were married. He has since passed away."

"No problem, Madame," the bellhop replied with professional detachment. "Take your time. Look around. The restaurant is down the path to your right."

I knew exactly where it was. The sights, sounds, smells and feelings all transported me back in time. Like two films spliced together, the past felt superimposed on the present. It was not quite mid-day and the heat was already mounting, but a gentle breeze drifted through the formal entranceway, cooling my skin. I loved the Balinese style of indoor/outdoor living. On my first visit, Bob and I were greeted warmly by the hotel staff who handed each of us a cocktail with a large purple orchid. Our energy was restored from the long trip as we sipped the fruity nectar and admired the surroundings.

Neither Bob nor I had ever been to such an extravagant resort. A thatched roof protected against the downpours that occurred most days. Dark teak beams met light polished marble flooring. Ceiling fans and rattan sofas all created an elegant yet comfortable atmosphere. Balinese music played in the background. The foyer had a single wall behind the sandstone check-in counter. A large bowl of white frangipanis on the counter brought me back to the day Bob and I checked into the resort just before our wedding. I remember watching him with pride as he leaned over the counter and joked with the receptionist. He had a knack for immediately making people feel at ease.

From the edge of the reception building, the property dropped off as a steep hill towards the ocean. Standing on the top of the stone steps, I could see lush vegetation surrounding generously spaced villas. The beauty of the resort, its swimming pools and winding paths were accentuated by the glistening turquoise ocean. The sight took my breath away and reminded me of Bob's excitement when he first stood there. "Check this out, Lianne," he said, eager to show me the spectacular view. It was as if time had stood still in the resort's entranceway. Nothing had changed in the dozen years since I was last there. The bittersweet memories of my time with Bob in Bali caused tears to well up.

"Mommy, please don't cry," Kerrsen said, bringing me back to reality.

"Yes, it makes us sad," chimed Kaiden.

"I don't think I will be able to do that," I tried to explain. "This is where your Dad and I were married. I am going to have to work through some tough emotions. Don't worry, though. I am okay. This is just something I need to do."

We walked down the stone steps through the property, the boys racing around as I was absorbed by my past reverie. I wished I was a painter. I could have depicted my memory and preserved it for all time. Instead I had to settle for my mind's eye. I saw the main dining area where we had our small wedding reception. I could see Bob laughing with my parents. My friend Martine was discussing with the waiter how to decanter the twenty-five-year-old bottle of wine that I had brought to Bali for the special occasion. She was particularly invested in it because we had picked up the bottle during a trip we did together in Portugal ten years earlier. My other friend, Cheryl, sat quietly, delighting in the moment. I was beaming with a serene happiness. As I recalled my younger self being surrounded with so much love and attention from my new husband, my parents and close friends, I suddenly felt terribly alone. There was this heaviness in my chest as I reflected on my current situation of raising two children on my own, while trying to heal from a devastating loss.

"Come on, boys." I tried to reel back my playful children from disturbing the other guests. "Let's go see the place where Daddy and I were married."

I led them down a winding path to a pagoda on a bluff jutting over the Indian Ocean. The pagoda was set up as a peaceful resting spot with comfortable sofas and tables, surrounded by hanging vines and flowering trees. From here we could see the local fishermen casting nets by hand into waist-high water.

Watching these men brought me back to our wedding day. Almost dusk, there were dozens of fishing boats spread out on the calm ocean below the cliff where we stood. My father and I sat side by side in a golf cart with orange marigolds teeming from its roof. This was our version of going down the aisle together. The second cart delivered my groom, my mom and our two witnesses. We all stood awestruck at the beauty of the view. The sun neared the horizon. Balinese umbrellas surrounded the pagoda in triple tiers of bright red, blue and yellow. The pagoda had been transformed into a small temple with dozens of the same orange marigolds hanging from its ceiling. White frangipanis sat in a silver dish on a table covered in white linen so that only a portion of its red and gold batik legs showed.

The minister dressed in white flowing robes greeted the wedding party and placed each of us in our spot for the ceremony. Bob squeezed my hand as the minister conducted the proceedings in a thick Balinese accent.

"Lianne, do you take Bob to be you husband, to love, honor and cherish as long as you both shall live?"

"I DO!" I couldn't be more emphatic.

"Bob, do you take Lianne to be your wife, to love, honor and cherish as long as you both shall live?"

"I do," he replied as he looked deep into my eyes with such love.

"Now, would you both like to exchange vows as you place the rings on each other's fingers?"

I choked back tears of happiness. "Bob, all of my life, my heart had been searching for you. The day we met was the first day it found true peace. I found my soulmate in you. And, on this day, I give you my heart and all of my love for eternity."

"Lianne, you have completed my life." Bob's voice shook with emotion, his eyes teary. "With you, I am a better person, and I will love you forever." We exchanged simple gold wedding bands each inscribed with: Love will keep us alive.

After the ceremony, we all sipped champagne, took photos and happily chatted. Bob and I took a moment, arm in arm, to look out at the ocean as the sun fell beyond the horizon. In the dark blue sea lay the mysteries of the future before us.

When we returned to our villa, Bob carried me over the stone threshold. Balinese music softly played on speakers. While we were at our ceremony, the staff had transformed our villa into a sacred matrimonial oasis. We held hands as our eyes soaked up the beauty. The canopied outdoor dining areas had crisp white linens and fine china. Champagne and various appetizers had been laid out around a floral centerpiece. Straight ahead of us, the infinity pool overlooking the ocean was filled with hundreds of frangipani petals dancing with the glimmer of tall white candles surrounding the space.

In our sleeping quarters a large white gossamer net covered the king-size bed. Yellow petals were sprinkled across the linen bedspread. Resting in the middle was another arrangement of frangipanis in a dish and a note from the hotel congratulating us on our marriage. After absorbing the beauty, Bob walked over to the CD player and inserted a new disc. He took my hand and led me back outside by the candlelit pool. "May I have this dance?"

Our first dance was to our song by the Eagles: *Love Will Keep*

Us Alive. Don Henley's hauntingly beautiful voice filled the air, reminding us that we had overcome so much to be together and would continue to survive as long as we had love in our hearts.

The sound of one of my boys giggling as they searched for lizards in the rocks above me pulled me back to the present. As the memory of our dance faded, I heard Bob's voice as a distant whisper in my mind reassuring me that love will keep us alive. It occurred to me that no matter what my future held, my love for Bob – the love we still shared – would help the boys and me to thrive.

I walked down the stone stairs towards the ocean. It was high tide so the small beach at the bottom was submerged. I stood on the lowest rung and released his ashes into the water. Filled with immense sadness and gratitude, I said aloud: "Goodbye, my love. Thank you for the wonderful life we had together. I give you my heart and all of my love for eternity." At that moment, a huge wave crashed against the rocks. I smiled, as I knew that it was Bob's way of saying "ditto."

"Look Mom, there's a huge monitor lizard," my boys cried excitedly. They hadn't been very interested in my trip down memory lane. Nor did they want to have anything to do with spreading their father's ashes. I guess this was one part of the trip I was meant to do alone.

The rest of the trip we spent touring around and exploring the idea of living in Bali. We went to visit the Green School and it exceeded my highest expectations. The setting was spectacular in the middle of the jungle. The curriculum was rich and diverse. There appeared to be a close-knit community of families originating from around the world. Kerrsen was excited about the idea of moving to Bali, but Kaiden was most definitely not. To my surprise, I was not that thrilled either. I asked many parents from the Green School why they chose to live near it and what they liked most about it. As I listened to their answers, it struck me that what they found in Bali, I already had at home: a strong community, beautiful nature, a slower pace of life, and an opportunity to pursue a spiritual path. I felt like Dorothy from *The Wonderful Wizard of Oz* realizing there is no place like home.

I had ventured to the other side of the world only to discover that the place the boys and I needed to be was back in Canada. Through this experience, I learned the valuable lesson that I lived exactly where I had to be to heal. I also was able to close a chapter in my story with Bob. I felt that revisiting Bali and the special place where we had married was a turning point. It wasn't that I was a painter with a blank canvas, as I originally thought, but rather a sculptor with large chunks of existing clay from which to mold my life. I was not creating my new reality from scratch, but a base of forty-six years and perhaps many past life experiences. This clay held all of my passions, wisdom, ideas, strengths and gifts, as well as purpose, opportunities, and soul longings. I didn't have to throw away everything that I held sacred: family, friends, community and work I loved. I could also remove or add chunks of clay to continue to form my life masterpiece. And, I didn't have to get it right the first time. I could work on my life as much as I liked.

On the plane ride home, I looked down at the wedding ring still on my finger. I knew I had to take it off to truly close this chapter of my life. The simple gold band represented all that I had loved and cherished. I didn't want to remove it. I thought of a compromise. I could put it on Bob's gold necklace that I wore with his wedding ring. This would keep the ring close to me and next to his ring. When I removed the ring from my finger and placed it on the necklace, it slid down the chain to meet the other ring. To my amazement, my ring didn't just rest next to Bob's on the chain, but nestled inside it. A perfect fit! Without any effort on my part the two rings slid together to form one.

CHAPTER 16

Love Will Keep Us Alive

Returning from Bali, I had renewed energy, a new lease on life. Through the teachings of the ancient and contemporary wisdom traditions that I had been studying before I left, I learned that all aspects of our lives – good and bad – are part of a larger blueprint. Sometimes, the hardest lessons help us to evolve the most. I heard someone say, "Never let a good crisis go to waste." This resonated with me. If Bob's death was part of a grand plan, I certainly didn't want him to have died in vain. I was motivated to transform my experience and new knowledge to create a new path for my life and work that would involve helping others. I wasn't sure how I would do this, but I felt I owed it to Bob to discover this new purpose of my own.

I was called to share the new awareness that was dawning in my life. It's hard to explain exactly why. My awakening was reminiscent of the early stages of my relationship with Bob when

I felt a shift from a black-and-white world to one full of color and vibrancy. This time it felt like my world had shifted into focus, as it does in the morning when I put on my glasses.

I wanted others to experience this. I began by sharing my newly formed beliefs and recent experiences with family and friends, as well as writing about them on my blog and other social media. It was scary. I worried about what people would think. I feared their judgment and disapproval, and even worse, that they would eventually cut me out of their lives.

That's exactly what happened with many people. Not all at once, but over time I noticed a pattern: invitations to parties and other gatherings became fewer. I wasn't sure whether this was people's unease with widowhood or with me sharing my new thinking. I also felt Bob's family, particularly his kids, drifting away from me since his death. He had been the glue. I desperately wanted them to remain a part of our lives for our boys, and because I felt close to Bob in their presence. I longed for their approval.

As much as I wanted to fit in with others, I began to realize that some of my old relationships no longer fit me. I grew bored and occasionally even annoyed with superficial chitchat. I questioned myself constantly. *Should I just go back to the way things were and not say anything? It would be so much easier.* There were times when I did keep quiet. One evening at a friend's house, the members of my book club were bemoaning the idea of having to look after their husbands into old age. I had to leave the room before I chastised them for not relishing the opportunity of growing old with their spouses. They had years to enjoy with their husbands — to raise their children together, travel the world, and possibly support one another in their later years. They realized their inadvertent insensitivity when they saw the sadness in my face and quickly changed the subject. I felt I was pulling them down.

For a while I only spoke openly with the people I trusted to listen to my beliefs without judgment. I was able to be more vulnerable with them and have deeper discussions. I was encouraged over time to see that by daring to be open with them, they became comfortable enough to share a bit more of their ideas and feelings as well.

I couldn't go back to the way things were in terms of my work either. I dreaded returning to the frenetic corporate world, but I was starting to worry about money. *How much longer can I live off my savings?* I was asked by one of my long-time clients to run a series of strategic planning sessions for the company's digital division. This involved helping the company's managers to clarify their new vision, assess the gap between where they were and wanted to be, and develop a plan and strategies to get to their goals. It was pretty typical of the work I had done for this and other clients in the past. I debated for days over whether to accept the assignment, feeling that if I agreed I would be selling out on my promise to make the most of my life going forward. I sought a compromise, hoping that by applying some of the new mindfulness practices in business, I might be able to integrate what I had been learning in my spiritual pursuits into the corporate world. I agreed to do the project if I could take a non-traditional approach. Trusting me after I'd worked for her on and off for six years, my client agreed.

In a large boardroom, I led a team of thirty department managers through my newly devised approach. I started with a guided meditation. I felt the discomfort in the room as people shifted in their seats and cleared their throats. I sensed a discreet collective sigh of relief when the meditation ended, as if they were thinking: *Phew, that's over! Now can we can get on to regular business?* But I wasn't finished with them. The next part of my plan was to do away with the normal process diagrams in favor of storytelling to redesign their business. These practices are now quite common in business, but were unwelcomed when I first suggested them. I realized later that I was ahead of the times. My client ended the project and never contacted me again.

Shunned in my professional and personal life, I became disheartened. I didn't know what to do, but I knew that I couldn't go back to my old life. It didn't fit me anymore.

With no work or clear path for my career and the distancing of Bob's family and numerous friends, I felt utterly alone. The day-to-day responsibilities of looking after my young children and caring for a large household by myself weighed heavily on me. My mother and siblings were spread across North America and unable to readily help. Access to child care was extremely limited because we lived in a rural area. One of my worst experiences was at the time of the H1N1 outbreak. Kerrsen developed flu-like symptoms that made me fear that he had contracted the virus. I needed to pick up medicine for him along with some groceries, but he was too sick to accompany me and too young to be left at home alone. I couldn't ask a friend to stay with him because there was so much fear about being exposed to the virus at the time. The dilemma took me to a breaking point. I felt unable to do the simplest things to look after my child properly. I was angry at Bob and at God for putting me in such an impossible situation. I knew it was crazy to blame them, but I needed to fault someone. With no other choice, I left Kerrsen with Kaiden, who was far too young to babysit, and fearfully raced to the store, frantically running up and down the aisles so I could return home as fast as possible. Everything was fine, but I felt a new level of isolation. *There is no one but me. I have to do everything alone.*

Loneliness and grief were my constant companions, only leaving me while I slept. Keeping busy with household activities and researching a new career path kept my grief somewhat at bay at times during the week. The slower pace of the weekends intensified the grief. Weekends had been dedicated family time before Bob died. We had only accepted social invitations that included us as a couple or the entire family. We had often held dinner parties for our friends, but I couldn't bring myself to host alone. Few invitations came my way. Week after week, month after month, I stayed at home alone with my boys. I began to look forward to Mondays. That was when my Spirit Circle would gather to meditate and hold spiritual discussions. Over time, however, it also became a source of discontentment. At each gathering before meditation, my friends would recount the events of their weekend with their families and friends. I often dropped hints that I would love to be included but hardly any invitations were extended. I couldn't understand why. Anger and resentment clouded my thoughts. *If they know how I feel, why don't they do something to help me?* Figuring I wasn't being open enough with them, I finally shared with these closest friends that I was extremely lonely on weekends and would really appreciate the occasional Saturday or Sunday invitation. Because I was close to a breaking point, I think my pleadings came across as needy and even judgmental.

Most of the responses stunned me. The majority of these friends cited family obligations and other reasons why they weren't able to have me and my boys over on a weekend. Instead, they offered suggestions. "Why don't you try to make new friends?" "What about new projects?" "Maybe it's time to find a new man!" These recommendations felt like salt in my wounds. While one good friend in particular kept me from giving up all hope, it wasn't enough to mitigate the hurt of daring to be vulnerable and being politely but nevertheless rejected. Not wanting to feel vulnerable had been the main reason that I avoided requesting help in the past.

Now I felt ashamed for vocalizing my needs and angry at the responses I had received. I was humbled to discover once again that I had not progressed as far on my spiritual path as I had thought. After all the personal development work I had done, I still couldn't read most people correctly and had mistakenly exposed my frailties. After that, I shut everyone out, creating a deeper sense of loneliness than I had ever experienced in my life. Grief compounded on grief as I withdrew from the Spirit Circle and distanced myself from many of my closest friends. The sadness and despair I felt were second only to the loss I experienced when Bob died.

To ease my suffering, I returned to my familiar coping mechanisms of meditation, journaling and connecting with nature. During my long walks in the woods, the thought occurred to me that if there was a purpose to everything, then there must be a purpose to this and I had to find it. I asked for insight. I sensed that I needed to journey on my own for a little while. I kept hearing the words *resilience training* in my head. In some native traditions, adolescents are encouraged to embark on a solitary journey, often in nature, as a way to put their character to the test and discover their own path in life. These vision quests are similarly found in other spiritual traditions. Jesus and Buddha each spent time in meditative solitude before returning to their communities. Why not me too? I sensed that any reliance on others, and even on my own victim story, were hindering me from moving forward. It was time for me to learn how to really tap into my own resources. I sought comfort in the one connection I knew would never fail me. I returned to my journal and began writing. "Bob, this is so difficult. How do I stop feeling such pain?"

"Pray. Change your thoughts. Find acceptance and forgiveness instead of focusing on the anger and rejection. Draw on your courage and insight. These are great gifts, not to be taken lightly. Self-reliance comes from your strength and stubborn nature. Acceptance comes from your insight about the bigger picture."

"Thanks, but what is the bigger picture?"

"Your friends are helping you to evolve. They will learn from this, too, each in their own way. What you want now and have been looking for all of your life is what everyone wants:

unconditional love and acceptance. By coming to an acceptance of your friends in this situation, understanding they are doing the best they can, you will begin to find acceptance of your own life, relationships and, most importantly, yourself."

"Maybe so, but this is easier said than done."

"This is about seeing people as they really are beyond their physical body and their personality, beyond the roles they play and the words they say. When all that is stripped away and we see each other as we really are at our core, we experience a connection that is sacred and enduring. You and I have that. You thought you lost it when I died, but it is not outside you. True love resides within you as your connection to the Great Source of All Things Divine. I, or rather our relationship, served as a mirror for you to see it. This journey is about you finding your way back to yourself, to rediscover the Divine Love within you."

"So, you're saying that I've been looking for love in all the wrong places?"

I felt like Dorothy from *The Wonderful Wizard of Oz* again, discovering that I'd never left home or rather home had never left me. In this case, home was a metaphorical place residing within me: my connection to wisdom, inspiration and creativity... to my soul. I had spent most of my life, especially in the years following Bob's death, seeking answers outside myself, when all along they were right there within me. I felt a euphoric rush of clarity pulse through my being.

"If all the answers are within me, and you are part of me, and I am part of you, what was the purpose of your death?"

"Well, that is a complex question. One person has an impact

on so many others. We are like dominoes: we affect not only the ones around us but hundreds, thousands, if not millions, of souls down the line. So, yes, my death is part of a larger blueprint that was planned to affect my loved ones... you, the boys, my other children, my brothers and my mother, but also numerous others.

"This is a time of great awakening on the planet. We had agreed before we were born that if we didn't awaken on our own when the shift was starting to take place that we would need a catalyst. And, if one of us were to leave, it should be me. You had a better chance of raising the boys alone. Also, it is the sacred feminine energy of compassion, acceptance and connection that is awakening in humanity. That is why so many women are the early risers, so to speak. As we approached the time of the great shift, it became apparent that a catalyst was needed. You had received one with your father dying. You reignited your spiritual path at that point and you started to gather a group of women around you. You sent out a strong message of desire to the Universe to go deeper and to integrate this into your life in a more significant way. Do you remember?"

"Yes, I do. I remember I was so excited and inspired when I read books and discussed spiritual concepts with others, but all of it felt fleeting. Within a few hours or days, I was right back into regular life. *How can I make this a bigger part of my everyday reality?* I remember asking myself."

"Well, that was a tipping point. That was the asking, the predetermined call that launched the course of actions for your spiritual awakening. As I said, this was earlier agreed upon. Our relationship was never bound by human laws, physical constraints or linear time. Our partnership is about the evolution of our souls. My illness and death occurred when they were appropriate for our mutual evolution. Our relationship represents a new kind of partnership — one that is designed to assist in spiritual growth. This kind of partnership will one day replace the traditional concepts of marriage bound by vows and obligations.

"I am simplifying things a bit, because my death also affected my other loved ones. Imagine a large web. What I am describing to you is only part of the web. It is your section, but my other loved ones, like our boys, each have their own sections. They, too, came into this physical reality with the desire to master some life lessons. It's the opportunity to awaken, but there are other important lessons as well. For Kerrsen, the lesson is self-reliance and compassion. He is a smart, strong, courageous soul. Losing his father at such a young age was one of the most difficult tests of his mettle. He will have the opportunity in his lifetime to teach others the important lesson of moving beyond deep sadness, loss and fear – of withstanding life's difficult blows. It has also helped to develop a sense of compassion within him.

"Kaiden is a very independent soul, like his mother. He needed an open environment. Growing up with you offers him the best way to avoid society's conditioning. Because of my own deep conditioning, I may have unwittingly squelched his unique gifts and life's mission. He will learn to stand up for his own ideals and develop his unique, independent voice which may differ from many or all of those around him. It won't bother him to be the lone voice in a crowd. This will be his way of instigating change."

All of this made a lot of sense to me. I couldn't imagine why other people would suffer needlessly for a situation that only affected me. "If we are all connected, not just the ones who are physical, but non-physical beings as well, is your death and my awakening part of your own ascension?"

"Bravo! You're getting this stuff! What you're saying is true for many loved ones who are non-physical at this moment, as well as other spiritual guides. We are experiencing through you the Great Ascension. We just have different seats from you at the show. While you are experiencing it in a limited way through your five senses, we have a broader perspective, but we don't get to experience it sensually the way you do. Either way, however, we are all expanding our individual and collective awareness. I feel honored to be experiencing it with you."

"Me, too. Thank you so much for accompanying me. If you don't mind, I would like to explore a little more how your death was my catalyst. Were there any other easier paths that I could have taken?"

"Yes, of course. We are given many ways to fulfill our mission during our lifetime. Do you remember when I had the operation and then went through cancer treatment and we both were amazed when the doctors found no visible signs of cancer afterwards?"

"Yes, how could I forget?"

"At that point, you and I could have chosen another course for our lives. You may remember that other things were falling apart at that same time. The economy went into a recession and your business took a tailspin. At this point you started to investigate living more consciously and doing some kind of different work. You — actually both of us — were afraid of the unknown and longed for the comfort of what was familiar to us. We even said that we just wanted to go back to our old life. That was like hitting the snooze button on an alarm clock. Life was trying to wake us, but we resisted."

"Yes, I remember that clearly. The same thing happened years earlier when you had an issue with your thyroid. Are you telling me that if we had taken a different path at that time, you might still be here today?"

"The answer to that question is not that straightforward. Again, there are many souls involved. But the simple answer is: yes, there could have been an easier way for you and me. This is an important message. We can always change our fate, even at the very last moment, as death approaches. That's why there are near-death experiences. While our souls repeatedly call our attention to lessons that we need to learn, they are subtle at first. If we don't listen, the message becomes louder until we are forced to listen. You sensed that you have been faced with this scenario of one of us leaving the other previously, maybe even multiple times. This is true, but this is the first lifetime in which you are truly mastering the lesson."

"Well, I guess that's good, but what is the lesson I am mastering?"

"Ah, that is for you to discover! But, I can tell you this: Love is all there is. Love is the purpose of life. How we each express love in our own unique way is our work in the world. This is why we both loved the song, *Love Will Keep Us Alive*. The song's message resonated with us on so many levels. First, the love we shared was the one constant that allowed us to weather each and every storm we faced together. In the beginning of our relationship, when we struggled against all odds to be together, it was our unwavering love that propelled us forward. And when life's challenges beat us down, like the difficult start to our relationship and then the lost jobs, moving to a new home, as well as the difficulties of blending families and raising children, it was our love that kept us happy and open to new solutions that would ensure we continued to thrive. Even when I became sick and died, it was our love that kept us connected and the love of our family and friends that have kept you going.

"Also, when we are aligned with love, we are fully alive. The idea of awakening is about living to one's full potential, living life in full bloom. Love is like the fine thread that attaches us all together. Again, I am referring to unconditional love. As we move away from a world of separateness, we are moving towards oneness. People are beginning to understand that all humans, living beings and even what we perceive to be inanimate objects are part of the one grand tapestry. We are moving into an age when humans consciously see themselves as part of this tapestry. While each square has its unique place and design – beautiful on its own – it is part of a much larger collective which, when seen as a whole, is much more spectacular than any one piece. Binding all the pieces are the threads of love.

"When we see ourselves as a separate section, rather than as an important part of this magnificent tapestry, we are not living to our full potential. More people are awakening to this larger picture. They are beginning to see themselves as an essential part of the overall tapestry. The key to moving from the perspective of the individual section to the perspective of the tapestry is unconditional love and surrender. It's realizing this greater connection and feeling this loving oneness that gives us true acceptance, courage and strength, as well as access to unlimited wisdom. However, it all starts with unconditional self-love. That has been your journey. Learning to love ourselves is what will keep us all alive."

"Wow! I see that now. Ever since I arrived on this planet, I've been seeking love and approval from everyone else, when true love is an inside job. I need to learn to love and accept myself as I am, and as I am evolving into better versions of myself, stumbling along the way. This is a huge realization for me. I am not sure how exactly I will do this, but I know with your help, I will persevere. So, where do we go from here, Bob?"

"We keep moving forward, ever expanding together. I can see you doing that now. You are finally completing this book of ours. Your work is on the right track. You continue to heal and reach new levels of awakening. This is a great blessing, and I am so happy for you. It is time for you to enjoy your life again — all of it. Don't worry. I will always be here to help you and the boys."

"I still miss you so much, but the pain is lessening. I am starting to feel whole again."

"Enjoy the ride, my love. You deserve it. We will be together again soon enough. And, remember: love will keep us alive."

Several years later, my phone woke me before dawn. As I stumbled half-asleep in the dark to reach my cell, the call went to voicemail. I was about to go back to sleep when Kerrsen entered my room to tell me that an alarm had been ringing for several minutes and had just stopped. I must have been in a deep sleep, because I never heard the alarm. When I went to investigate, I discovered that the door to the garage had opened ever so slightly, tripping the alarm. After I called the alarm company to report the false alarm, I listened to the voicemail message left by the alarm service. The message took me by surprise: "November 23rd, 4 a.m., Robert Parkinson, you have an alarm situation. Please call us immediately." This was one of the only service accounts that I hadn't bothered changing to my name after Bob died. When I heard the date and time, followed by his name, it dawned on me that this was not random, but a message from beyond. I had completely forgotten that day would have been our seventeenth wedding anniversary. Hearing this message, connected to Bob's name, and the time, 4:00 a.m., confirmed to me that it was him reminding me. As I hung up the phone, I turned to Kerrsen and laughed. "That was your Dad, wishing me a happy anniversary!"

I continue to feel Bob's presence as he sends me gentle, often humorous and sometimes dramatic reminders that he is still very much with us, guiding me and our boys, along our path together. I now take what I've learned and experienced to share with others. First to help them realize that life continues beyond our physical existence and that there is a whole universe or multiverse for us to explore. In the past, my vision was restricted to the finite, material world. My understanding of the soul's journey through this lifetime and many others had been limited. Now this vision is ever expanding and the daily unfolding is delicious. I discovered a truth that had been hidden from me for the longest time: we are energy, co-creating life at each moment and, as such, have infinite potential. With this huge opportunity comes the responsibility to direct the unfolding of our soul's calling in a way that not only betters our own life, but creates a ripple effect of positive change in the world.

It has taken me a while to get to this point, but I can truly say that I am grateful for this journey. While losing Bob was the most difficult experience I've ever gone through, it also redefined my life in almost every way — deepening the connection to my inner wisdom and the nurturing beauty of self-love. Losing the love of my life helped me learn to find my own worthiness and independence and to reorient my compass towards my true north. Life has shown me that I am here to help others do the same: to awaken to their life purpose and passions and realize the interconnectedness of all things. My life's mission is to help others uncover their unique soul's expression and to translate it into their contribution towards improving the world. Today, I am driven to help others to live as I do: inspired, filled with meaning and joy, and relishing the nourishing abundance of evolution.

About the Author

Lianne Bridges is an inspirational change leader, author, coach and international speaker who is driven to help others reignite their passion and discover their deeper calling. She believes that when we're connected to our purpose, we harness the power to transform worlds, starting with our own. Her memoir, *Love Will Keep Us Alive*, recounts her journey of awakening to her life's purpose.

She caught the entrepreneurial bug in 1999, when she launched a successful marketing business. Her world shattered at forty-six when she lost her husband to cancer. Her profound grief prompted her to rethink her entire life. She closed her business and went on a journey of healing and self-discovery, immersing herself in personal development teachings and spiritual practices. She sensed that her time on Earth was about more than being successful in her own right.

Lianne decided to put her MBA and 30-year track record working for multinationals in service for others. In 2009, she founded Designing Transformation Productions, which supports individuals, business owners and leaders to awaken to their potential through vision, self-empowerment and alignment with their purpose.

You can email Lianne at contact@designingtransformation.com, or visit her on one of these sites:

Web: DesigningTransformation.com

Facebook: www.facebook.com/designingtransformation

Twitter: twitter.com/Liannebridges

Instagram: www.instagram.com/designingtransformation/